Women,
the Earth,
the Divine

ECOLOGY AND JUSTICE

An Orbis Series on Global Ecology

Advisor Board Members
Mary Evelyn Tucker
John Grim
Leonardo Boff
Sean McDonagh

The Orbis Series *Ecology and Justice* publishes books that seek to integrate an understanding of the Earth as an interconnected life system with concerns for just and sustainable social systems that benefit the entire Earth. Books in the Series concentrate on ways to:

- reexamine the human-earth relationship in light of contemporary cosmological thought
- develop visions of common life marked by ecological integrity and social justice
- expand on the work of those who are developing such fields as ecotheology, ecojustice, environmental ethics, ecofemnism, deep ecology, social ecology, bioregionalism, and animal rights
- promote inclusive participative strategies that enhance the struggle of the Earth's voiceless poor for justice
- deepen appreciation for and expand dialogue between religious traditions on the issue of ecology
- encourage spiritual discipline, social engagement, and the reform of religion and society toward these ends.

Viewing the present moment as a time for responsible creativity, the Series seeks authors who speak to ecojustice concerns and who bring into dialogue perspectives from the Christian community, from the worlds' religions, from secular and scientific circles, and from new paradigms of thought and action.

Also in the series

John B. Cobb, Jr., *Sustainability: Economics, Ecology and Justice*
Charles Pinches and Jay B. McDaniel, editors, *Good News for Animals?*
Frederick Ferné, *Hellfire and Lightning Rods*
Ruben L.F. Habito, *Healing Breath: Zen Spirituality for a Wounded Earth*

ECOLOGY AND JUSTICE SERIES

Women, the Earth, the Divine

Eleanor Rae

ORBIS BOOKS

Maryknoll, New York 10545

BT
83.55
. R34
1994

The Catholic Foreign Mission Society of America (Maryknoll) recruits and trains people for overseas missionary service. Through Orbis Books, Maryknoll aims to foster the international dialogue that is essential to mission. The books published, however, reflect the opinions of their authors and are not meant to represent the official position of the society.

Library of Congress Cataloging-in-Publication Data

Rae, Eleanor.
    Women, the earth, the divine / Eleanor Rae.
        p.   cm. — (Ecology and justice series)
    Includes bibliographical references and index.
    ISBN 0-88344-952-8 (pbk.)
    1. Feminist theology.   2. Feminity of God.   3. Ecofeminism.
I. Title.   II. Series: Ecology and justice.
BT83.55.R34   1994
230'.082—dc20   93-47614
                                                     CIP

Printed on recycled paper

TO EVA STELLA
My Mother

Contents

Acknowledgments

The writing of this book has been a mostly solitary process of several years duration. This makes the interaction with colleagues, family, and friends all the more valuable and valued.

Literally, this book could not have been written without that great institution, the public library. Through the Ridgefield, Connecticut, library and the interlibrary loan expertise of Jacqueline Valentino, there was no corner of the world that was not made accessible to me. This expertise and devotion to her work was also evident in the typing and management of the manuscript provided by Paula Hand, with whom I have enjoyed a long and productive relationship. I owe a warm thank you to Jay McDaniel, who provided the initial opening to Orbis Books for me. The manuscript itself was improved by the criticism of its Introduction and 5th chapter by the Mid-Hudson Women in Theology Group (WITS), founded by Regina Bechtle and Kathleen O'Connor. The months of lonely struggle were compensated for by the enthusism with which my editor at Orbis, Bill Burrows, received my work. To Mary Evelyn Tucker, I owe much gratitude for the loving and careful way in which she criticized and enabled me to improve my manuscript. And a bridge between writing and lived spirituality was provided by the women who gathered at the Center for Women, the Earth, the Divine on the second Saturdays of the month. A particular thank you is given to Margaret Parente, who translated my themes into living ritual, and Jacqueline Vacheron, who helped us translate the theme into meaning in our own lives. And to Grace Burford and Susan Postal, who enlightened me in areas of Hinduism and Buddhism respectively. Finally, where would any of us be without family and friends, both human and nonhuman? I thank Her for making all of these gifts part of my life. I must say that through it all, She gave me the very strong sense that the book was being written because She wanted it to be written!

Introduction

The 1990s are commonly viewed as the time when the human species on Earth will deal in a serious manner with the ecological crisis—because it has no other choice. A high point of this decade was to have been the United Nations Conference on Environment and Development held in Brazil in 1992. At this Earth Summit the heads of state of the world's nations were to have to gathered and, as a body, addressed this crisis which affects all that makes up the Earth's body as well as the space through which we travel. But the Earth Summit has come and gone, leaving in its wake little hope that we will act out of a common vision for the Earth's well-being; rather, we have shifted almost overnight from seeing the world in terms of an East-West conflict to seeing it in terms of a North-South confrontation. The play is the same; the only difference is some shifting of players and scenery. But if the dialogue did not take place among the heads of state, it can still take place among those of us who do strive for a world vision. Such dialogue can bring about the needed changes, but these changes will take place only if all the critical elements are taken into consideration. As Elizabeth Janeway has so succinctly stated: "When things are stable, the world can run on the basis of limited input; not when the skies are falling."[1] For me, as well as many other women and men, the key element that must be included in the dialogue, if real and needed change is to occur, is the reclaiming of the feminine.

Reclaiming the Feminine

While the feminine is not limited in its context, there are nevertheless certain key places where it is most appropriately rediscovered. These are in women, in the Earth, and in the Divinity. These three, both factually and symbolically, offer us the deepest insights into the meaning of the feminine. These insights are being perceived not only by Western peoples, but also in the East. As Vandana Shiva writes: "The violence to nature as symptomatized by the ecological crisis, and the violence to women, as symptomatized by their subjugation and exploitation, arise from *this subjugation of the feminine principle.*"[2] Further, Shiva sees this feminine principle as embodied, not only in women and the Earth, but also in *Prakrti*, the source of all life.[3]

1

Elements initially associated with the feminine, and with women and nature, include activity, productivity, and creativity.[4] These are physical qualities which are discernable in the quantitative universe. In addition, I would posit the qualitative element of non-conditional love as this love is demonstrated through the actions of women, the Earth, and the Divine.[5] While it is possible to attempt to exploit the non-conditional love of women and the Earth, this cannot be done without serious consequences to all the participants. From the perspective of a process theologian, one could also argue that it is possible to affect the Divine giver of non-conditional love. What cannot be affected is the giver's decision to love non-conditionally. Symbolically, this embodiment of the feminine finds its initial expression in the Great Goddess, the One who was revered in ancient times in much the same way as people today revere and image God.[6]

What is needed today is for women both to look within themselves and to come together in order to define what the feminine is. It is no longer acceptable — if, indeed, it ever was — for the definition of the feminine to come out of a patriarchical world-view. When I look within myself for the meaning of the feminine, the first thing that strikes me is how much my understanding has changed over the years. For much of my life, I lived as if I were a disembodied spirit. I think that, if I had awakened one morning to find my body gone, I would not have missed it. But gradually my attitude toward my body has changed and is still changing. I now take very seriously the fact that everything we know is embodied, including possibly the Divinity.[7] And, while I would agree with the position that sees the feminine and the masculine being a continuum rather than as two totally separate and self-contained entities, I nevertheless would argue for a distinction between them that can be characterized as masculine and as feminine.[8] This conviction comes, not from study, but from six decades of living. It seems to be how the Divine Artist has fashioned much of creation.

An additional valuable place to look for the articulated expression of the feminine is in the feminist movement, which Marilyn French characterizes as "the only serious, coherent, and universal philosophy that offers an alternative to patriarchal thinking and structures."[9] Specifically, in this book I will look at the articulation of the feminine from the prospective of the ecofeminists and in the light of the specific contribution that Christianity particularly, and the other major world religions, can make to ecofeminism.[10] My purpose is not primarily to critique the past; it is rather to provide momentum for the movement into a viable future.

Making the Connection: Women/the Earth

The word *ecofeminism* has not yet made its way into the subject matter and catalogues in the libraries I have visited. But, judging by the growing body of literature being produced in this area, it will soon be found there.

While this is encouraging and important, the reality is that, in the environmental movement itself, there is still a lack of awareness on the part of most ecologists of the women/Earth connection. As Ynestra King states:

> For the most part, ecologists, with their concern for nonhuman nature, have yet to understand that they have a particular stake in ending the domination of women. They do not understand that a central reason for woman's oppression is her association with the despised nature they are so concerned about.[11]

Yet there is little reason why this lack of understanding should exist. The women/Earth connection is being articulated not only by ecofeminist philosophers such as King, but also by people from disciplines as far-ranging as economics, the physical sciences, theology, and archaeology.

A former member of the New Zealand parliament, Marilyn Waring, has researched the economic condition of the world's women. Her conclusion is that the economic systems worldwide treat both women and the Earth in fundamentally the same way: as invisible and valueless — and there for men's free use.[12] Likewise, Maria Mies in *Women: The Last Colony* argues persuasively that women and subjugated peoples are treated as if they were means of production or natural resources, similar to water, air, and land. For Mies, the economic logic behind this colonization is that women (as the means of production for producing people) and land are goods that can in no way be produced by capital. Control over women and land is, therefore, the foundation of any system based on exploitation. What is paramount is to *possess* these means of production; the relationship with them must therefore be one of *appropriation*.[13] Or, as Shiva would express the relationship, women are initially devalued because their work cooperates with nature's processes and, secondly, because work which satisfies basic needs and ensures sustenance (the requirements of nature) is devalued in general.[14]

While the above-mentioned writers look at women and the Earth through an economic focus, Carolyn Merchant sees the same pattern of domination but as a result of the Western scientific revolution. For Merchant, there is an association between women and nature that has persisted in culture, history, and language, and that is grounded in a world-view which may be characterized as egalitarian. Nature and women are further linked by the ancient thinking that regarded nature as the nurturing mother.[15] After the Western scientific revolution, the image of nature (and women) as wild and uncontrollable, rather than nurturing mother, became the predominant one. Out of this understanding grew the need to control totally that which was no longer valued on its own terms.[16]

Still others, such as Rosemary Ruether, make the connection between the imaging and treatment of women and the Earth through the discipline of theology. Ruether sees in patriarchy and its transcendent sky gods the creation of a dualism which emphasizes the finitude of both women and nature while aligning the male with immortality and the male god in whose image he is created. This patriarchal dualism stands in strong contrast to the time when all—heaven and earth, gods and humans—were seen as part of the maternal matrix of being.[17] While the debate still rages on how much historicity we can impute to the existence of a matricentric age which preceded the present patriarchal age, there are those who present well-documented evidence concerning these prehistorical times as an age when women and the Earth were seen in similar ways—but in ways that were positive rather than negative.[18]

But whatever the outcome of the debate on the prehistorical evidence, none of us can afford to lose sight of the fact that changes have occurred in the world through thousands of years or of the fact that some of these changes were created by human beings. This leads us to conclude that humans can alter the way we think and live now and in the future.[19]

The Ecological Crisis as a Religious Issue

In 1967, Lynn White, Jr., argued that the root cause of the ecological crisis could be found in the Western attitude toward nature, fostered by the Jewish and Christian traditions, that nature's only purpose for existing was to serve humankind.[20] He contended: "Since the roots of our trouble are so largely religious, the remedy must also be essentially religious."[21] This perception of the ecological crisis as a religious issue is shared by many who are not necessarily connected to institutional religion.[22]

The earliest roots of ecology as a religious issue can be seen in the matricentric age with its ubiquitous presence of the Great Goddess. Minimally, the presence of the Great Goddess symbolized an understanding of all of creation as being part of the mystery of life—a mystery which held within itself the elements of death and of regeneration as well as fertility.

With the shift from the matricentric to the patriarchal world-view, worship came to be focused no longer on the giver of life, death, and regeneration but on the sky gods who had control over nature but were not a part of it.[23] Men came to identify themselves with these gods, if not actually, at least "*symbolically* through the creation of a self-image supported by law, theology, philosophy, and through the creation of lower classes."[24] As evidenced in the major world religions and our secular institutions, it appears that this world-view is still with us.[25]

It may be argued that even those who no longer worship the gods explicitly are still under their influence. For example, Eli Sagan speaks of the ritual human sacrifice that is going on in modern societies today:

> The fact is that our secular twentieth-century democracy maintains the need to sacrifice some to the angry gods, whether it is the slaughter

of the president in the public-opinion polls, or the periodic ritual homicide of our young men in wars to save the world for something or from something, or the persistent, unrelenting degradation of one class of people whose means for "pursuing happiness" are consistently being taken away. Thinking we are free, we may be more in the hands of an angry god than ever.[26]

He goes on to speak of the 1980 presidential election, where a leading candidate boasted publicly about the way to win a nuclear war with the Soviets. He says, "If you asked such a man if he would buy a slave and slaughter him in order to assure electoral success, he would look at you as if you were insane, and yet he seemed willing to sacrifice more than half the people in the world for 'victory.' "[27] And what of our willingness to sacrifice women and children today, when we have the ability to feed them and prevent them from dying from certain diseases? Are we not practicing human sacrifice? Are we not still, as Sagan says, under the power of an angry god?

Finally, for me personally, the ecological crisis is a religious issue because of the question of ultimate value. As a Christian theist, there is only one place where I can posit ultimate value and that is in the Divinity. Further, one of the values that I believe has ultimacy is that of the feminine. So I am faced with this need to posit the feminine in the Divinity, but within a religious tradition which leaves little room for such placement.[28] The working out of this issue is part of the third section of the book, along with looking at other world religions to consider how they treat the issue of the feminine in an ultimate way.

The Organization of This Book

"The Present Situation of Women," Chapter 1, looks at the origin of women's present historical situation and examines the possible responses to this situation. The specific response in the United States of America is then examined. The chapter concludes by setting forth aspects of the diversity and the unity of the response to the present status of women.

In Chapter 2, "Ecofeminism," we examine the meaning of ecofeminism. Then we look at some issues that have surfaced in the discussions of ecofeminism. These include the relationship between women and nature, and the philosophical issues of instrumentalism, dualism, complementarity, and unity/diversity.

"Living the Earth-centered Future Today" — Chapter 3 — examines what this lived experience looks like in terms of values, ethics, transformation, bioregionalism, and green politics.

Chapter 4, "Toward a Contemporary Cosmology," looks at the relationship among myth, mysticism, and science, as well as the relationship between modern science and cosmology. We look at the Universe as the body of the Divinity and begin the telling of the new story of the Universe.

In Chapter 5, "The Holy Spirit as the Feminine Divine," we look at the issue of the Christian Divinity as feminine. A beginning theology of the Holy Spirit is presented under the categories of Her work, Her relationship to the Word, Her relationships within the Trinity, and Her Person.

The concluding chapter, "The Feminine and the Major World Religions," examines the relationship between the feminine and the major world religions of Hinduism, Judaism, Buddhism, and Islam.

The Epilogue is a glimpse of the Black African Buffalo on the plains of the Serengeti.

PART 1

WOMEN

1.

The Present Situation of Women

The International Women's Year was declared by the United Nations in 1975. It ushered in the International Women's Decade, a decade which was to rectify the situation that showed that women did two-thirds of the world's work, received 10 percent of all income and owned 1 percent of the means of production. However, rather than improving during the decade, the situation of women worsened. A document produced by an independent group of researchers at the end of the decade stated:

> The almost uniform conclusion of the Decade's research is that with a few exceptions, women's relative access to economic resources, incomes and employment has worsened, their burden of work has increased, and their relative and even absolute health, nutritional and educational status has declined.[1]

It would appear that this poverty is serving as the "great equalizer," in that the situation of women in the so-called developed world and that in the developing world is drawing closer all the time.[2] But if this is the worldwide situation of women today, we might ask ourselves if it was always like this and, if not, what conditions led to the present abysmal situation of most of the world's women.

Origin of Women's Present Situation

While the issue of whether or not there was a time when women enjoyed a status equal to, or possibly even superior to, that of men remains to be resolved, the evidence that such a time actually did exist is accumulating. We are hampered in deciphering the evidence for this matricentric age because it comes to us not by way of written language, but through the artifacts out of which archeologists carefully construct their case. Ultimately, what is being attempted is to elicit an understanding of the whole

9

culture of a people. Thus, for example, Marija Gimbutas used approximately two thousand symbolic artifacts—dated from primarily 7000 B.C.E. to 3500 B.C.E. (later in the West) and found in Old Europe (the area between the Atlantic Ocean and the Dnieper)—as the basis for her work on the language of the Great Goddess.[3] Joseph Campbell compares her work to that of Champollion's decipherment of the Rosetta Stone—and more, for on the basis of her decipherment, she has established "the main lines and themes of a religion in veneration, both of the universe as the living body of a Goddess-Mother Creator, and of all the living things within it as partaking of her divinity."[4] These symbols, which "represent the grammar and syntax of a kind of meta-language," enable us to enter the world-view of the culture of Old Europe.[5] This culture Gimbutas characterizes as egalitarian, nonviolent, Earth-centered, and matrilineal.[6] In *The Language of the Goddess*, Gimbutas presents the Great Goddess in her four major aspects: as life-giver, as eternal Earth mother, as death giver-regeneratrix, and as energy.

Women and men from other disciplines, relying on the findings of the archaeologists, have seen in their findings a reason to accord to women who lived in the time when the Great Goddess was worshiped a social prestige which is not theirs today. Thus, for example, social theorist Murray Bookchin argues that "the presence of female figurines, obviously laden with magical or religious significance, in the debris of a prehistoric hunting camp or a Neolithic horticultural village suggests the reasonable probability that the community accorded women a social prestige that would be difficult to find in the patriarchal societies of pastoral nomads."[7] Futurist Riane Eisler also sees the link between the worship of the Great Goddess and the status of women. She describes how, with the Kurgan invasions, the Goddess was reduced to wife or consort of the male deities, while women were "gradually reduced to the status they are to hold hereafter: male-controlled technologies of production and reproduction."[8] And art historian Merlin Stone sees in the great energy exerted by patriarchy to hide or deny the almost universal existence of a female clergy that existed when the Great Goddess was reverenced, evidence that Her image did indeed affect the perception and status of womanhood.[9]

In conclusion, it may be said that since myth explains, justifies, and reinforces the existing social reality, any change in the social reality must be justified through changing the myths. The acceptance of a particular world-view must ultimately take place within the individual. This dialectical process between myth and social organization which took place with the creation of patriarchy is described by Bookchin in the following terms:

> The most complete shift occurred in the psychic apparatus of the individual. Even as the Mother Goddess continued to occupy a foremost place in mythology (but often adorned with the demonic traits required by patriarchy), women began to lose whatever parity they

had with men—a change that occurred not only in their social status but in the very view they held of themselves. Both in home and economy, the social division of labor shed its traditional egalitarian features and acquired an increasingly hierarchical form. Man staked out a claim for the superiority of his work over woman's; later, the craftsman asserted his superiority over the food cultivator; finally, the thinker affirmed his sovereignty over the workers. Hierarchy established itself not only objectively, in the real, workaday world, but also subjectively, in the individual unconscious. Percolating into virtually every realm of experience, it has assimilated the syntax of everyday discourse—the very relationship between subject and object, humanity and nature. Difference was recast from its traditional status as unity in diversity into a linear system of separate, increasingly antagonistic powers—a system validated by all the resources of religion, morality, and philosophy.[10]

While the above describes what the process of change looked like, it does not describe what caused this shift from seeing women and men in terms of "unity in diversity" to seeing them in hierarchical terms. The obvious biological differences seemed to have played (play) a part, but dominance based on biological differences alone is contradicted by the fact that the study of tribal people today indicates that male dominance is not a universal phenomenon.[11] For example, Peggy Reeves Sanday's work strongly suggests that it is possible to have a sexual division of labor within an egalitarian context.[12] Thus, it may well be that the correct question is not, When did the sexual division of labor originate? The answer to that question is obvious. But rather, the questions should be, How did this division of labor become a relationship of dominance and exploitation, and why did this relationship become asymmetric and hierarchical?[13] Sanday sees male dominance as the result of stress: either internal, as, for example, in famine, or external, as, for example, in warfare.[14] On the positive side, she argues that if the system that "defines and gives direction to a people's life . . . develops in the absence of forces threatening social survival, women wield economic and political power or authority and the power relationship between the sexes is balanced."[15] The results of her studies of tribal peoples indicate a correlation between:

female supernatural symbolism	male supernatural symbolism
cooperation	competition
sexually integrated tasks	sexually segregated tasks
inner/plant gathering and cultivation	outer/animal hunting
joint child care	absence of male parent[16]

But while a case can be made for emotions such as stress and fear being the bases of sexual inequality, one must also ask if there are not also positive values that enter into the equation and provide bases for choice in a given social context? Further, if this is in fact the reality, what is the nature of those primary ethical values? These questions will be addressed when we look at the ecofeminist critique of patriarchy in Chapter 2 and in the treatment of the values issue in Chapter 3. For our present purposes, having presented some possibilities for the origins of women's present historical situation, it is now time to look at some of the responses that may be given to this reality.

Possible Responses to Women's Historical Situation

If one takes seriously the present situation of women, it seems that a response to this situation is required. Then the issue becomes, What kind of a response is appropriate? While it is possible simply to remain a man-defined woman in a man's world, the role into which most women have been socialized, it seems that this would occur only if one rejects the reality of woman's situation. An alterative response, if one has the ability, is to become a "man" in this world, a high-powered "token" who is able to do everything that men do—and do it even better. The problem is that the admission of such women to the male society will do little to change this society or to better the lot of their sisters who may not be as bright and talented.[17] Or, if one takes seriously the need to change both self and society, then the need to become a self-defined woman calls for recognition. From the Christian perspective, this involves the recognition that I am created in Her image and that within me exists the power to be what a woman is. This is the work of at least a lifetime. The choice is clear and irrevocable while the path is admittedly difficult. The question then becomes, Do I interact with the world as reformer or as revolutionary? But before I can act at all, I need to be convinced that I have the power to bring about change and, even more basically, that power has a positive rather than a negative value.

For many people, the term *power* does in fact carry a negative value. Yet, in its dictionary definition, it is neither negative nor positive; it simply means "to be able."[18] It is how power is used that gives to it its positive or negative value. Marilyn French argues that power in its negative form has become the dominant value of the Western world. Power in its negative form may be translated as "control over." This new value of "control over" replaced old values such as fertility, continuation, and sharing.[19] To see how French's insights are presented in our times, we need look only at our history books and our media. There we see celebrated the men (it is usually men) who control the most: people, territory, ideas, wealth.[20] The goals of control are limitless; it cannot have an end, as there is no degree of control that can be enough.[21] However, this way of thinking contains within itself an inherent contradiction, because we live in a world of finite resources.

Where this ultimately leads we see today as we stand on the brink of losing our life-giving elements of air, soil, water, without which no one can survive. Jürgen Moltmann argues that the male justified his acquisition of power (control over) by seeing power as the primary attribute of God. Man did this so that he might achieve his own divinity.[22] He could have seen other attributes as primary, such as beauty, truth, goodness, wisdom.

Rather than having a negative valve, power—"to be able"—also can be used in a positive way. It can be used to enable rather than to control; thus it would be power "for," rather than power "over." From the Christian perspective, it may be seen that a recurring theme in both Testaments is the identification of the Holy Spirit with power. For example, Micah 3:8 reads: "But as for me, I am filled with power, with the Spirit of the Lord, with authority and with might, to declare to Jacob his crimes and to Israel his sins." And throughout the Christian scriptures, but especially in Paul and Luke (1 Thes 1:5; Rom 15:19; Lk 1:35, 4:14; Acts 1:8, 10:38), we find the identification of power with the Holy Spirit. To present just one example, Acts 1:8 reads: "You will receive power when the Holy Spirit comes down upon you; then you are to be my witnesses in Jerusalem, throughout Judea and Samaria, yes, even to the end of the earth."[23] According to the gospel of Mark, we live in the Holy One's field of power (dynamis) and for this reason our actions are good; the one who trusts and believes has the Holy One's power.[24]

In summary, we may say that, as well as being negative, power can also be positive. As well as power which is hostile to life (life being the gift of the Spirit), there is also power which enhances and gives life, power which co-creates with the Spirit. While we may acknowledge that this power is needed more than ever to shift the balance from death to life, on a practical level we may ask what women, who have often experienced themselves as powerless, can do.[25] We can begin by using what Elizabeth Janeway calls the powers of the weak.

For Janeway, the first power of the weak is their ability to question the strong. This can move us from acquiescing to the agenda of the strong to a withdrawal of our consent regarding the actions of those who govern. Our power is based on the fact that it is the weak who give the strong legitimacy.[26] In other words, for Janeway, power is an interdependent relationship between the governors and the governed. It is a process and not a thing. She sees the charismatic leader as answerable, not to a Divine authority, but to the governed alone. This occurs because power is based in the community.[27] Further, if we give total responsibility to the governors, what we are doing is "arranging" to see them as betraying us if anything goes wrong."[28]

History gives us many examples of women who questioned authority. It may be said that the Civil Rights Movement in the United States began when Rosa Parks questioned authority and refused to give up her seat on the bus. At a more distant time, the reformers in Scotland mark the start of their reformation from the time a woman in St. Giles Cathedral in Edinburgh picked up her stool and threw it at the sermonizer. The prophetic action of one person in questioning authority seems capable of starting a whole movement for justice. Even Eve is now being seen in a positive sense as one who questioned authority and brought knowledge to the human race.[29]

The second of Janeway's powers of the weak is their ability to come together, to form groups, and to choose their own goals.[30] While she acknowledges that "the weak who withdraw from participation in active life weaken the powerful by diminishing the number of active followers," she further states that "they weaken themselves even more."[31] She identifies the action that follows dissent (the thought process) as consisting of the identification of common interests and the establishment of a separate system. This process calls for both mutuality and structure.[32] Eleanor Haney says much the same in her proposal for revolution. For Haney, what is needed is the formation of alliances—alliances that not only effect political change but are a sign of what they say; the setting of the group's own agenda by the group itself, which can only be accomplished if there is clarity of vision, the ability to see all aspects of a given issue, and the establishment of goals; and the transference of power, that is to say, the ability to both resist the status quo and to create alternatives.[33]

Janeway addresses the issue of ritualizing, not as a separate issue, but as a part of the group-gathering process. Because of its significance, however, I envision ritual on its own terms. As Janeway herself says, it is the function of ritual to publicly declare "the significance of the event it celebrates and of the group that meets to carry out the ceremony."[34] It is also the function of ritual "to call up and renew mutuality."[35] Through good ritual—ritual which is in touch with reality—the participants actually can be transformed. The need for empowering ritual explains in part the current movement known as Women-Church.[36] Haney summarizes this power of transformation when she says:

> We can be open to the power of transformation, celebrate it, use it, be changed by it. It is in the sun and the atom, the seed and ocean, the cat lying beside me, in love and friendship and sexuality, in organizing and action, in healing, in worship and celebration, in civil disobedience and creating alternative structures. As we exercise power, it is increasingly revealed to others. As they see and live it, it surges across the globe in waves of cool blue-green water flecked with foam, cleansing, tearing down, and re-creating.[37]

Finally, I would propose a fourth element of the powers of the weak, and that is our power to create a vision to undergrid and motivate our thinking, acting, and ritualizing. One of the advantages that the weak have at this time in history is that the vision does not have to be particular to one group; rather, it can be shared by all of humankind. The story of the Universe, which we will look at in Chapter 4, is the story of each and every one of us—human and nonhuman alike. We are all primarily recycled stardust. But as well as cosmology, our vision can be inspired by earthly sciences such as zoology and physics. For instance, Moltmann points out that, against a competitive model, Russian zoologists demonstrated as early as 1880 that "it is precisely those beings that live symbiotically which prove to be the strongest."[38] Or, following French, we can look at the world of subatomic physics, a world which she characterizes as fluid, transient, eternal, many-sided, and nonhierarchical, where things work by attraction and the negative has its place. Based on this model, order without dominance is a possibility; entities can be both self-directed and interconnected.[39]

There are three elements which say the vision can become a reality. First, there is our understanding that we can change. The human is not something fixed but something in process. The human is becoming. Second, we are all related to all that exists. We are all part of one physical-spiritual reality. Third, we have the ability to implement the vision. We have power.[40] We need not be limited even by our imaginations for, if we are willing, we can go to places we cannot now even imagine.

*

The Response in the United States of America

In this section on the response of women to their historical situation, I wish to limit myself to only one country, the United States of America, and only one issue, that of racism. (In the next two sections, I will discuss the response of women in a wider context both geographically and in regard to diversities such as nations, religions, and races.) I do this because, as a women who is a citizen of the United States, I cannot help but respond to the pain that the issue of racism is inflicting on women in this country. For me, this is epitomized by the reality that some black women have found it necessary to separate themselves from the feminist movement and become part of the womanist movement. At issue is how we can work together to save the Earth. Divided, we will not save our World.

It seems that women's concern for civil rights—an initial but in many ways now-questioned phase of the feminist movement—first surfaced in a highly idealized way. As Elise Boulding states:

> The deliberate campaign by women to obtain civic rights did not begin systematically until the 1800's and it began as a by-product of their own efforts. It was only when they were handicapped in their work for schools, for the poor, for control of conditions of emigration for woman, and in their campaigns against slavery and alcoholism—handicapped because of their legal status as females—that they finally were pushed into fighting long-overlooked limitations.[41]

For those in the Christian fold, at least, feminism could be viewed as part of the great movement for liberation of which anti-slavery was also a part. This could be summed up in a text such as Galatians 3:28 which states: "There is neither Jew nor Greek, there is neither slave nor free, there is neither male nor female; for you are all one in Christ Jesus."[42] But it seems that for some, at least, the parts did not carry equal weight but were seen as primary and secondary. This inequality was observed by Sojourner Truth, who at the Equal Rights Association Convention held in 1867 observed:

> There is a great stir about colored men getting their rights, but not a word about colored women; and if colored men get their rights, and not colored women theirs, you see the colored men will be masters over the women, and it will be just as bad as it was before.[43]

This same ability to look at women as second-class citizens within the Civil Rights Movement may also be observed in more recent times. Thus, there was opposition to seeing women as part of Title VII because, in the view of some of those in the movement: "Women were well off and should not be allowed to compete with minority groups."[44] Jo Freeman goes on to note: "Ironically, it was overcoming the hostility of civil rights activists, not congress, that was the first major battle of the new feminist movement. In fact, this hostility was a major contributor to the formation of the movement."[45]

During the 1980s some black feminists began to view the feminist movement as controlled by white, middle, or upper class, college educated women. bell hooks has even gone as far as to characterize its thrust as the relieving of the boredom of housewives through obtaining employment outside the home.[46] While I think it could be argued that hooks's interpretation is too narrow, I do think she is correct in her perception that the movement must expand in order to better meet the needs of non-white women and working-class women. But in order to do this, we must recognize the issue of classism as well as racism, evidenced by, for example, the making of exclusive black upper-class enclaves of previously exclusive white clubs in former colonized countries, or, at the more fundamental level, the oppression that black governments inflict on black peoples in some African countries.[47] I think our hope rests in honoring our diversity, whether of race or religion or age, and yet being in touch with the reality that, at a still more basic level, we share the experience of being women. This is our primary source of strength and revelation. Out of this source there is the need to move beyond the human to see the Earth itself and all of its creatures as deserving of participating fully in the mystery of Life.

The Uniqueness of the Response: Diversity

Gloria Joseph acknowledges the dilemma that black women face when she speaks of black women having "at least as much in common with black men as with white women."[48] This exemplifies the problems that each woman must face because she is not simply a woman, but a woman from a particular racial background; a woman from a particular religious tradition; or more, a woman from a particular economic stratum. These problems are not easily resolved. As a woman who claims my privileged educational status and the heritage of my Polish peasant parents, I sometimes find that in honoring one dimension, I may be betraying another.[49] Nor is this true for Western women alone. Leila Ahmed contends that Muslim women are also faced with this issue of conflicting loyalties; if one is true to one's "womaness," one is false to Islam, while if one if true to Islam, one is false to one's "womaness." Ahmed sees the issue in terms of personal loyalty *vs.* cultural betrayal or personal betrayal *vs.* cultural loyalty. She sees the issue as further compounded for Muslim women in that many perceive feminism as a Western import.[50]

How the religious aspect that women claim is experienced around the world accounts in part for our great diversity. While all "the great religions of the world (of both East and West) uphold similar principles as far as the submission of women to men is concerned," how this reality is incultured varies widely.[51] Thus, for example, Fatima Mernissi argues that Muslin women are placed under male domination because women are feared as sexually powerful, while in the West women are viewed as inferior because they are considered biologically inferior.[52] She sees Muslim society as not so much opposed to the equality of women as to the heterosexual unit, because this unit would get in the way of man's relationship to Allah by providing love, loyalty, and so on.[53] Within this framework of reasoning, it follows that men and women are taught to be enemies.[54]

In the West, women often seem to conspire in their own submission in that they have internalized a sense of worthlessness. In her study on the nature of female sinfulness, Valerie Saiving Goldstein sees male theologians as identifying "sin with self-assertion and love with selflessness."[55] In contrast, Goldstein perceives woman's sin as

> Underdevelopment or negation of the self. [This is lived out as] triviality, distractibility, and diffuseness; lack of an organizing center or focus; dependence on others for one's own self-definition; tolerance at the expense of standards of excellence; inabilities to respect the boundaries of privacy; sentimentality, gossipy sociability, and mistrust of reason.[56]

While some of the particulars of how women present their lack of self-esteem to the world may have changed in the 1980s and 1990s, it seems that seeing themselves as valueless is still a common experience.[57]

I would argue that there is a positive correlation between women's personal perception/social situation and the imaging of the Divinity as feminine.[58] However, the issue is much more complex than simply admitting goddesses into a pantheon or positing a feminine aspect of a monotheistic Divinity. In fact, the presence of a feminine Divinity can be utilized against women rather than for them. This appears to be the case with the Goddess in Hinduism in that some males so fear re-engulfment with the female or become so fixated on the Goddess that they project their fears onto women. Thus, on the religious plane they are seen as adoring the Goddess, while on the human plane they are misogynists.[59] Nevertheless, there are also instances where it can be shown that the worship of the Goddess has had a positive effect on women.

In the Indian province of Bengal there is strong evidence that points to a positive correlation between the social status of women and the popularity of Goddess worship.[60] Likewise, a contemporary study has been done concerning the status of women on Cheju Island in Korea where the Goddess is worshiped. The theologians who conducted the study concluded: "As evaluating the goddess image of Cheju Island and its function in connection with the social life of Cheju women, we found the image has a close correlation(s) with the important role of the women's economical activities, that is not like other areas of Korea."[61] And, while Goddess worship may no longer be a part of the experience of Arabic women, Nawal el Saadawi states:

> The important position occupied by some goddesses was symbolic of the relatively higher prestige enjoyed by women in Arab tribal society, and a reflection of the vestiges of matriarchal society that still lived on in some of the tribes.[62]

Besides the freedom to worship the Divinity in its feminine aspect, although in diverse ways, a sense of self-worth may be effected by the laws of a given culture. A recurring theme in a series of articles written by seven Eastern and nine Western participants of a June 1990 trip to China was the sense of self-esteem Chinese Christian church women seemed to enjoy. This self-worth seemed to be based in part on the equality which is theirs by law—defined in the Chinese constitution and Mao Zedong's understanding that "women held up half the sky." However, they also noted that law does not always translate into lived experience.[63] What is worthy of note for our purposes here, however, is that the positive self-image of these women comes not from their religious experience of being Christian, but rather from their legal and ideological status.

As well as race and religion being factors in the worldwide diversity that women experience, I would like to look at economic factors as contributing to that diversity. In this instance, I will look at women who are part of the economy of one third-world country—India—and discuss the contribution that these women are making to our understanding of the ecological crisis. To place this contribution in context, we need to contrast the economic struggles which are faced by the "developing" countries with those which

are faced by the "developed" countries. For the former, the threat to survival is immediate for the majority, while the minority experiences economic
growth which is both resource wasteful and resource intensive. For the
latter, the struggle is between short-term over-production and over-con-
sumption and long-term survival options.[64] Further, we need to distinguish
between two kinds of poverty: what Vandana Shiva calls *real poverty* and
describes as the misery of deprivation, where basic needs are not being
met, and *culturally perceived poverty*, in which one's basic needs are met.[65]
As the providers of sustenance, third-world women are linked to nature,
not only biologically, but also culturally and historically.[66] This recognition
of women and nature as the producers of life has two consequences. First,
what the West calls development is really destruction, or what Shiva calls,
maldevelopment. This is not happenstance; nor is it, therefore, something
that readily can be corrected. Rather, it is rooted in the patriarchal assumptions of domination, homogeneity, and centralization. Second, the solution
to the crisis has to come from outside the patriarchal model. Shiva suggests
third-world women as the source for the creative solution; village women
do not have the patriarchal world-view.[67]

Specifically, Shiva sees the women and tribal peoples of India as the
natural scientists of the world. They are its sylviculturalists, its agriculturalists, and managers of its water resources.[68] In all of these roles, women
take a holistic approach rather than a reductionist one. Thus, for example,
the forest is seen "in terms of water, herbs, tubers, fodder, fertilizer, fuel,
debris, and as a gene-pool," and not merely as a source of timber.[69] The
women of the Chipko movement understood the ecosystem and acted out
of this understanding for they knew that without the trees there is no water
and there is no soil.[70] As food producers, women employ the feminine
principle based on the intimate links among trees, animals, and crops, and
on the work of women in maintaining these links.[71] They employ the principle of recycling, which "provides the necessary inputs for seeds, soil mois-
ture, soil nutrients, and pest control."[72] Shiva calls this model self-
reproducing and sustainable, terminology also applicable to their understanding of the water cycle.[73] For women and tribal people, water is a
renewable but finite resource that continually beings forth life in its cycle
from sea to air to land to sea.[74] Women know it is nature and not male
technology which supplies water; water is the source of water.[75]

In summary, Shiva would characterize the world-view that is currently
operating not as development, but as maldevelopment in that it is causing
the death of nature and has left women with meaningless lives. She characterizes the principle out of which this world-view operates as masculinist
and reductionist—reductionist in that it sees the world only in terms of a
commodity market. She sees the need for a new world-view characterized
by the recovery of the feminine principle, the principle which sees life at
the center of the meaning of the world.

What Women Have in Common: Unity

Shiva's reaction to the destructive world-view is her call for the recovery of the feminine principle. This call is necessitated by the fact that we all, North or South, East or West, live in a world that is dominated by the ideology of patriarchy. This ideology adversely affects all women—and all men, other creatures, and the Earth itself. According to French, the ideology of patriarchy begins with a false theorem: that humanity is separate from nature. Building on this false hypothesis is a second principle, which bases this separation on men's kinship with a higher power. This higher power, which may be God or rationality or a hierarchical system, grants some men control over the rest of creation. Third, the ideology of patriarchy posits that the loss of control (power over) causes men to decline to the status of subhuman beings—like women, blacks, workers—or even possibly come under their control.[76]

French goes on to argue that patriarchy has deprived women of the fringe of life and its activities and pleasures, while it has deprived men of the core of life, which includes love and intimacy, pleasure, community, and sharing. Also, it has called the fringe the core, and vice versa. But women know better, and many men also know that they have been exiled from real satisfaction. French contends that efforts to extend the perimeters of either realm toward the other will fail as long as patriarchy continues to define men in opposition to an "other," whether the other is nature or women or other races.[77]

From a male point of view, Bookchin describes patriarchy as

the civil sphere of the male, who produces rationalized ceremonial and military systems as compensatory mechanisms for his own ambiv- alent status in organic society. He is necessarily less fulfilled in a domestic society, where woman forms the core of authentic social activity, than in a civil society—but one that he must elaborate into a fully articulated and structured sphere of life. His very identity is at stake in a world where production and reproduction are centered around woman, where the "magic" of life inheres in her own personal life-processes, where the rearing of the young, the organization of the home, and the fecundity of nature seem to be functions of her sexu- ality and personality. Whether he "envies" matricentricity or not is irrelevant; he must evolve an identity of his own which may reach its most warped expression in warfare, arrogance, and subjugation.[78]

Given the ideology and the lived experience of patriarchal society, Gerda Lerner argues persuasively that the reforms and legal changes which some women are experiencing within the patriarchal society give only an illusory and unwarranted sense of freedom. Rather, what is needed is that such reforms "be integrated within a vast cultural revolution in order to transform patriarchy and thus abolish it."[79]

But if all women share the experience of being oppressed by patriarchy, do we also share similar experiences out of which we can act to create a new world? The most obvious place to begin an affirmative answer to this question is with the acknowledgment of our embodiedness. We can see our bodies as a primary source of revelation and celebrate what this teaches us about ourselves and our interconnectedness to all of creation. This avenue of spirituality is open to all, whether relying on ancient religious traditions or not. Thus, to cite only one example among many, Penina V. Adelman develops rituals based on the Jewish lunar calendar; the calendar then serves as "a vehicle for noting the monthly cycles of women's fertility and understanding the female aspect of God."[80]

Further, women share the ability to dream and to envision. The power of the traditional religious stories, ideals, and images acknowledged by scholars of the Buddhist tradition (as well as other traditions) are a potent force for good or harm to women.[81] If women are to be effective agents of change, we must dream our own dreams and create our own visions, and not rely solely on those which are presented to us by males. Concretely, the power of the image can be seen in the fact that, while women in the German Democratic Republic enjoyed full equality under the law, they still had problems in the realms of self-identity and self-image. This would suggest that, long after our legal goals are met, we will not have reached our true goals—unless we change our vision.[82]

In addition to our embodiedness and our ability to create a new vision, we might consider the five traits that Devaki Jain suggest form "a critical core which is universal to all women."[83] These values are the desire for peace, a sense of care, the rejection of hierarchy, the capability for self-reliance, and a sense of tradition. She suggests that the feminist basis for social action would come out of the development of self-reliance and individual autonomy, which she characterizes not as rugged individualism, but as individual responsibility in the context of community.[84] I will cite two examples which make Jain's list concrete, examples chosen because they are found in places which a Western woman would characterize as unlikely and therefore add weight to the universality of these traits.

The first example pertains to Jain's principle of the rejection of hierarchy. Mernissi gives us this example from the Islamic world, where she says that the rigidity of the response as well as its violence is accounted for by the fact that the very foundation of the Muslim hierarchy is being destroyed by women who are claiming their power. In other words, in claiming their right to be individuals, these women shatter a rigid hierarchical world-view which limits itself to seeing men as slaves to Allah and masters of women, and women as slaves to men.[85] In regard to Jain's principle of the capacity for self-reliance, Mies gives us an example from India and its women's sangams. This movement of poor women was able to produce its own village-based leadership. The role of the woman from outside the village was that of coordinator rather than that of a leader espousing a particular ideology. Within this model, the village women could develop their own ideas and strategies based on their collective experience. In time, the men came to see that women's organizations strengthened, rather than weakened, the village's ability to achieve its goals.[86]

Based on the above, it appears that we have the necessary elements as far as an analysis of the true situation of women in the world is concerned and also in regard to what is needed to bring about a new world-view. But it also seems, at least in the USA, that we are living in a time of massive denial where we are retreating into the private sphere and refusing to acknowledge reality. What we need now is a critical number of people who will acknowledge reality and act out of this knowledge. The hope is that this action will not come too late.

2.

Ecofeminism

The actions described in the last chapter in regard to the poor women in India grew out of their deep understanding of the interrelationship of their own existence and that of the Earth of which they are a part. In fact, it is highly likely that this connection between the Earth and women first occurs on the intuitive level, not only in the East but in the West as well. These intuitions need to be lived out in the daily lives of people, but they also need to be articulated in order to change the consciousness in the peoples of the world. For our purposes, this developing change of consciousness is referred to by the term *ecofeminism*.

What Is Ecofeminism?

In its broadest sense, *ecofeminism* is the coming together of ecology and feminism—a coming together brought about by those who see the link between the domination of women and the domination of nature.[1] As Val Plumwood sums it up, this linkage results from the striking parallels which exist between the treatment of the Earth and the treatment of women. For example, the traditional role of both is seen as an instrumental one—women and the Earth are viewed in terms of having usefulness rather than as having intrinsic worth in their own right. Also, each occupies a sharply differentiated place in the hierarchical system.[2] But in addition to grasping an understanding of the parallel between the treatment of women and the Earth, ecofeminism also perceives these parallels on the conceptual level—the level of world-view, myth, symbol, idea, and image.

According to Carolyn Merchant, the term *ecofeminisme* was first used by Francoise d'Eaubonne in 1974 and signifies "women's potential for bringing about an ecological resolution to ensure human survival on the planet."[3] The paths which individuals traveled to reach an ecofeminist understanding are diverse, but at least three strands of these journeys by feminists have been identified. The first is through the study of political theory and cultural

23

history. Second, there is the journey through exposure to nature-based religion, a religion which specifically honors the female; its "scripture" is nature itself, and its focus is immanence rather than transcendence. Third, there is the involvement by feminists in environmental issues such as Green politics.[4] Chronologically, in the United States, it well may be that the first people to make the connection between ecological issues and feminism were community activists such as Rachel E. Bagby, Lois Gibbs, Carol Von Strom—people "who were struggling to protect the health of their families and neighborhoods."[5]

This praxis of feminism and ecology together may be viewed as a natural development in that both share common goals. Both see that all parts of the system—whether the human or nature—have equal value; when there is ethical conflict in the system, it must be resolved from the perspective of the good of the whole as well as from the perspective of the interconnectedness of all of the parts. Both feminists and ecologists regard the Earth's house and the human's house as habitats to be cherished; there is a need for these habitats to be life-sustaining rather than life-destroying. Both ecologists and feminists regard process as primary. All process takes place within the understanding that the total amount of energy leaving and entering the Earth is a constant; all the parts are engaged in a dynamic process of growth and development, death and decay, and their input into this process needs to be valued. Both understand that there is "no free lunch." This insight calls for cooperation and reciprocity rather than useless expended energy; all must return as much as possible to a system out of which they have taken.[6]

For Karen J. Warren, on the other hand, there are four insights that form the foundation for ecofeminism: that the oppression of women and the oppression of nature are deeply connected issues; that an adequate understanding of these twin oppressions calls for an understanding of the nature of these connections; that feminist theory and practice call for an ecological perspective; that ecological problems can be solved only if they include a feminist perspective.[7] In a similar vein, but from an expanded perspective, Ynestra King articulates four beliefs on which ecofeminist principles are based. They are, as in Warren, the close identification between the subjugation of women and of nature (Warren's 1 and 2) and the need to transform society according to ecological and feminist principles (Warren's 3 and 4). In addition, King stresses the interconnectedness of all of life and the critical need for diversity.[8]

In the future, we may expect to see the principles of ecofeminism developing and expanding. This is to be expected because ecofeminism is a new movement and therefore in process, but it is further true because the issue of process is at the heart of ecofeminism. However, within the boundaries of ecofeminism there are certain things which could not be included. Among these would be any of the "isms" of domination, such as sexism, naturism, racism, classism, heterosexism. On the positive side, it includes that which treats respectfully women's moral experiences and the interaction of the human and the nonhuman worlds.[9]

Based on insights taken from the Green experience, Lee Quinby also argues against a homogenic theory of ecofeminism. Quinby sees the strength of ecofeminism lying in its ability to have an impact in a multiplicity of places against specific power abuses; in this manner, it "not only weakens the junctures of power's networks, but also empowers those who do the struggling."[10] Thus, a *we* is formed around an issue, rather than around a politically correct theory. Ecofeminism in the interrogative mode asks difficult questions, not only of others, but of itself. Quinby suggests that "the we of ecofeminism is most formidable in its opposition to power when it challenges its own assumptions."[11] This questioning enables us to hear other voices—not only the human, but also those of factory farm animals, fish suffocating in polluted waters, and the flood waters rushing over deforested lands.[12]

Ecofeminism's ability to address the issue of power in its negative form of "power over" entails more than its ability to question the status quo and to develop coalitions around issues. Its strength also lies in the fact that it is a way of thinking; it is a philosophy that offers an alternative vision. Furthermore, its means and its end are identical; it increases the well-being of its adherents, which should appeal to all who see it; and it operates out of the present virtues of joy, community, and integrity.[13]

In the remainder of this chapter, we will look at some of the issues that have emerged as important to ecofeminism in the context of its being a philosophy. These include the relationship between women and nature, and the issues of instrumentalism, dualism, complementarity, and unity/diversity. In the following chapter we will examine how some of the values of ecofeminism are applied to Earth issues.

The Women/Nature Issue

Since the beginning of the human species, women have been very closely associated with nature. When the attitude toward nature is one of reverence and awe, this association works for women's benefit. When the attitude is one of rape and plunder, as it is today, this association does not benefit women. This shifting from a time when women and nature were honored and the divinity was immanent, to a time when men seek to control women and nature and the divinity is transcendent, is described by French in the following terms:

But because humans are not, were not, and cannot be in control of nature (within them or without), as the gods were imagined to be, they could attain their new status—humanness as control—only symbolically. Religious ritual and social arrangement created an appearance of—and sometimes real—control. And because of the age-old association of women with nature, the human race itself was stratified, with men taking the role of god, the human in control, and women taking the role of nature, the human who is controlled. This process comprises the origins of patriarchy.[14]

This scenario continues to be played out in the Hebrew scriptures where, for example, Elijah wins the contest with the priests of Ba'al when he proves that his god has more control over nature than do their gods (1 Kings 18). It is played out in Greek society, where

> Aeschylus' declaration that the father was the parent of the child and the mother mere vessel, like the earth in which the man plants the seed, was given theoretical, scientific validation by Aristotle who teaches that the sperm is merely nourished by menstrual blood to create the father's progeny. This was the final step in the defeat of the ancient world of matricentry—the usurpation by men of the one talent they do not share with women, the appropriation of procreation. It is a belief still current in many parts of the East and Middle East.[15]

We see this scenario played out in the present-day West where we speak of virgin timber and the rape of the land; where women are described as animals: chicks, foxes; where both women and nature are sometimes not dealt with because they are put on a pedestal.[16] And in the present-day East, where the patriarchal world-view understands destruction to be production, and the regeneration of life, in both nature and women, is viewed as passivity.[17]

Within the writings of the ecofeminists, the woman/nature issue often has been framed with the terms articulated by Sherry B. Ortner in 1974 in an article entitled "Is Female to Male as Nature Is to Culture?"[18] However, it is worth noting that this contemporary articulation of the women/nature connection goes back at least to the 1940s when, for example, Simone de Beauvoir "mentioned in passing the attitudes of men (under patriarchy) to nature and to women and the connection between the two."[19]

The writings around the women/nature equation fall into at least two categories. There are those which respond to the question directly, either negatively or positively. The negative response calls for the severance of the women/nature connection and the integration of women into culture. Those responding in this manner include Ortner herself as well as de Beauvoir. On the other hand, there are those who have chosen to reinforce and celebrate the women/nature connection. This reinforcement may take place in the context of an adversarial position toward men and patriarchal culture, as in the position of Mary Daly, or it may result in consciously choosing the women/nature connection as the basis for creating a whole new kind of culture, as in the position of Ynestra King.[20]

On the other hand, some writings have questioned the validity of the analogy itself. French thinks that the use of power over (control) would provide a better measurement of the diminished status of women and nature in societies. She sees this diminishment as highest where control is valued the most—even in those societies where men are associated with the wild (nature) and women with the tame (culture).[21]

Others have questioned not only the terms of the women/nature analogy, but the validity of the question itself. Catherine Roach argues that the question itself is wrong for two reasons. First, no beings can be closer to nature than any other beings; everything is simply part of nature. Second, the question perpetuates an environmentally unsound nature/culture dualism.[22] I add to Roach's observations a third point: the validity of the analogy can be called into question because culture itself cannot exist outside of nature.

If one chooses to respond positively to the women/nature connection, what might be some of the values and benefits of such a response? I will cite two examples, one based on the experiences of third-world women and the other from the North. We can learn from third-world women that production means the ability to bring forth life and sustenance and that it involves caring for nature—a care that demands the return of some of its resources to nature itself if it is to survive.[23] From the "developed" countries, we can learn from the ecofeminists who are using their power to speak for the "other" in both the Earth/human relationship and in the female/male relationship. As Judith Plant states:

> Ecofeminism, by speaking for both the original others, seeks to understand the interconnected roots of all domination as well as ways to resist and change. The ecofeminist's task is one of developing the ability to take the place of the other when considering the consequences of possible actions and ensuring that we do not forget that we are all part of one another.[24]

Obviously, women's most direct connection to nature is in our embodiedness. And here, even if the choice is to celebrate the connection, issues arise around which it is not always easy to put a positive light. Two of the most critical issues in this regard are those connected to reproduction and those connected to mothering.

The summation for the problems connected to reproduction, from an ecofeminist perspective, is presented succinctly by Beverly W. Harrison's statement that "the perpetuation of patriarchal control itself depended on wresting the power of procreation from women."[25] She would include in this the church's teaching on birth control and abortion. But if this is the problem, what insights does ecofeminism bring to the task of working toward a solution? Is what Patricia J. Mills characterizes as an abstract pro-nature stance of help here, particularly in the area of abortion? Mills argues that the pro-nature stance leads to contradiction with a pro-choice stance because if nature creates the pregnancy, then the human has no right to intervene.[26] But Mill's argument does not take into account the human's place in nature. Our pro-creative acts take place through choice as well as instinct. This being the case, it seems that we need to take the issue of non-conceiving more seriously than we do presently. An avenue we need to explore is not only our connectedness to nature but also our uniqueness as a species in nature's continuing enfolding.

The role of women—and men—as nurturers of children is also in need of creative insight from the ecofeminist perspective. As with the reproductive issues, the problem is quite evident. In this case, it is the way in which mothers function in a patriarchal society. If we narrow our focus to the time after the industrial revolution, we see that many women lost their productive functions and functioned only in the reproductive area. This reproductive area included the adjunct duties of physical and emotional nurturance of husband and children.[27] With the old feminisms concentrating on the need to put women back into productive functions, the negativity that surrounded the value of mothering often continued to flourish. What the ecofeminists need to offer today is a positive evaluation of the role of mothering (parenting), which, realistically, is the most important role that any human being can have, and some examples of positive role models for both dual parents and single parents who want to function in a manner which exemplifies a post-patriarchal society.

This post-patriarchal society would be based on the understanding that all are a part of nature. But it is not only the ecofeminists who have this encompassing world-view. This holistic world-view is also being articulated by those who refer to themselves as deep ecologists, a group with whom ecofeminists would appear to have much in common. The phrase *deep ecology*, coined by the Norwegian philosopher Arne Naess, is offered as a contrast to what he saw as the band-aid approach of "shallow environmentalism." Joanna Macy compares deep ecology to what is called by the Buddhists "the jeweled net of Indra." Broadening her description, Macy states:

> The perspective of deep ecology helps us to recognize our embeddedness in nature, overcoming our alienation from the rest of creation and regaining an attitude of reverence for all life forms. It can change the way that the self is experienced through a spontaneous process of ever-widening identification. It launches one on a process of self-realization, where the self to be realized extends further and further beyond the separate ego and includes more and more of the phenomenal world. In this process notions like "altruism" and "moral duty" are left behind.[28]

For Macy, this awareness is beyond external exhortation. Do we need to be told not to saw off our own leg? Then why do we need to be told not to saw down the trees of the Amazon rain forest—our external lungs?[29]

While there are obvious resonances between the thinking of a deep ecologist such as Joanna Macy and the ecofeminists, there are also deep disagreements. From the ecofeminist perspective, these center around the insight that the same consciousness that created the problems in the first place cannot be used to solve them; in other words, those who are deep ecologists are still coming out of a patriarchal mindset which has the male/female, masculinist/feminist dichotomy as a fundamental premise. It can be argued that women do not have to learn that they are part of nature; because of our biological properties—menstruation, pregnancy, birthing, and nurturance—we recognize ourselves as part of nature rather than as "other."[30]

A detailed attempt to examine the convergences and divergences of deep ecology and ecofeminism also acknowledges the premise that, while ecofeminists see patriarchy as the real source of the domination of nature, deep ecologists ignore this insight. So what structures and beliefs are responsible for our current destruction of the biosphere? According to deep ecologists, they are anthropocentrism, dualism, atomism, hierarchalism, rigid autonomy, and abstract rationalism. Further, it may be stated that we are in our present situation because of our mindset; that is, our unexamined presuppositions naturally bring us to the place where we are today.[31] As a result, deep ecologists would argue that

> only a revolution in humanity's understanding of itself and its place within nature will bring about the dramatic changes in human behavior that are necessary at this critical juncture in human and terrestrial history.[32]

Ecofeminists see the destructive role played by atomism, dualism, hierarchalism, rigid autonomy, and abstract rationality. However, they cite androcentrism (man-centeredness) and not anthropecentism (human-centeredness) as the key to the current destruction. For ecofeminists, patriarchy is the foundation for the other categories. Further, ecofeminists note that deep ecology has been hampered by the lack of women's voices in its development.[33]

As well as the issue of the "isms," at least one ecofeminist, Val Plumwood, would disagree with the deep ecologists over their understanding of the s(S)elf:

> It is unnecessary to adopt any of the strategems of deep ecology—the indistinguishable self, the expanded self, or the transpersonal self—in order to provide an alternative to anthropocentrism or human self-interest. This can be better done through the relational account

of self, which clearly recognizes the distinctness of nature but also our relationship and continuity with it.[34]

We will look in more depth at Plumwood's understanding of the relational self when we address possible solutions to our present-day crisis in the section on unity and diversity. But before looking at solutions, an analysis of the problem using the categories of instrumentalism and dualism will be presented.

Instrumentalism

According to Plumwood, one of the striking parallels between the treatment of nature and the treatment of women is that the traditional role of both is seen as an instrumental one. In other words, both are seen in terms of their usefulness to others rather than as having intrinsic worth in their own right.[35] In a later writing, Plumwood grounds her thesis on instrumentalism in a dualistically conceived dichotomy where differences are polarized and shared characteristics are minimized. In this dichotomy, differences are seen in terms of superior/inferior with the inferior viewed as a means to the higher ends of the superior. Further, in critiquing instrumentalism in the context of a critique of instrumental reason, Plumwood offers the three following observations. First, intrumentalism is strongly connected to a theory of discontinuity. Second, the existence of instrumentalism depends on a recognition of a sharp distinction between the sphere of means and the sphere of ends. Third, there is an understanding that that which is being treated instrumentally (women and nature) is passive and therefore lacking in ends of its own; this leaves the superior side free to impose its own ends.[36]

But what are the origins of this kind of rationalization? Taking the long view, one could certainly trace it back to the beginnings of the patriarchal age when, for example, people decided to use metal to make weapons, not only for self-defense, but for purposes of aggression. Instead, technology could have been limited to creativity involving the common good. At a more immediate time, it has been noted that the creation myth adopted by Christianity puts down not only women but also children (by their exclusion) and animals, plants, even nature itself. Men—and the male god—are free, according to scripture, to mistreat, sell, violate, sacrifice or kill women, children, plants, animals, and nature.[37] This instrumental way of thinking and acting can be seen accelerating through the centuries until, as Rosemary Ruether articulated so well in 1975:

Infinite demand incarnate in finite nature, in the form of infinite exploitation of the earth's resources for production, results in ecological disaster: the rapid eating up of the organic foundations of life under our feet in an effort to satisfy ever-growing appetites for goods. The matrix of being, which is no less the foundation of human being, is rapidly depleted. Within two centuries this pattern of thought and activity has brought humanity close to the brink of the destruction of the earth and its environment.[38]

It seems that we are dealing here with an equation that is relatively simple to comprehend—infinite expansion and demand on the one side *vs.* finite resources on the other—yet impossible to equate in reality. The fact that we still use the GNP as a form of measurement and still talk in terms of growth and development rather than sufficiency indicates that we have not understood the irrational nature of the equation.

The theme of instrumentalism is also the basis for an updated version of Rachel Carson's *Silent Spring*. In *The Recurring Silent Spring*, H. Patricia Hynes argues that, despite Carson's evidence concerning the poisons that we have introduced into the whole Earth cycle, we continue with business as usual. She says we rationalize this behavior because we see women and the Earth as there for man's use.[39] Each of us is experiencing this reality in our own lives: through the death of the song birds who are no longer there to wake us in the spring; through the death of the amphibians whose joyful behavior is no longer part of the life of our ponds; through the death of the farm workers who work directly with the poisons and all of us who are being poisoned slowly through the consumption of contaminated food.

Instrumentalism not only provides a context for an analysis of the poisoning of our food, but we can also look at the eating of animals as a form of instrumentalism. Ultimately, we see animals as being there, not for their own sakes, but to be used by us for food. Whether it is through the horror of "factory farming" or the "relational" hunt, where animals are killed with respect and appreciation for their sacrifice, we are still the moral agents who are responsible for the animal's death. Does this behavior honor the animal's life experience? Carol J. Adams sees a disparity between the eating of animals—a corporate problem—and the romanticizing of the "relational" hunt—an individual solution.[40] For Adams, the eating of animals is a participation in an ideology of dominance and power over; it is a failure to define the self in relational terms.[41]

Given the depth of the crisis that has arisen from our failure to define ourselves in relational terms, it is apparent that what we are looking for in the area of a solution is nothing less than a redefinition of the human. In this redefinition, both the distinctness and the connectedness of the human—as well as of all of the other participants of creation—must be held together in creative tension. The issue becomes: where does one look for a model that embodies this new consciousness? It would appear that it must somehow lie outside of the consciousness that has created the crisis. While in a real sense there is no place which is truly outside, on the other hand, there are whole populations, as well as individuals, who have participated less in the bringing about of the present crisis. These populations include the poor, indigenous people, and women. Some of the strengths that the poor bring to the new definition of self have been noted in the previous chapter, particularly as evidenced in present-day India. And slowly, in our own time, we are beginning to take note of the wisdom that is inherent in the relationship that some indigenous cultures have to the land — a relationship that may be characterized as not accidental but essential, so that the land is seen as "like brother and mother."[42] In the section on unity and diversity, we will examine how the relationship of women (and men) to nature can lead to a new definition of the human. But first we need to look deeper into an analysis of the crisis as it is seen through the category of dualism.

Dualism

According to the *Dictionary of Philosophy*, dualism is that "theory which admits in any given domain, two independent and mutually irreducible substances."[43] Key to the ecofeminist understanding of dualism is the placing of the substances in a hierarchical system, where one term would be regarded as normative and the other as derivative and/or defective. Among the many possible dualisms that could be examined, we will limit ourselves to the following sets to which ecofeminism has brought substantial insight: God and the world; creation and redemption; men and women; public and private.[44]

As explicated by Grace Jantzen, the basic theological dualism is what she refers to as cosmic dualism, the split between God and the World.[45] What is posited by this cosmic dualism is "a God of ultimate value and a material universe of no intrinsic worth."[46] This cosmic dualism comes out of our doctrine of creation ex nihilo, a doctrine that Jantzen says is not in the Bible. Rather, it is at odds with the biblical accounts, which show the divine Spirit forming Cosmos out of chaos. The dualism between God and the World is rather philosophical in its roots, coming from Plato and, more recently, Descartes. Theologically, it is grounded in teachers as diverse as Origen and Augustine, who held that man's creation in God's image pertained to his mind only and not to his body.[47]

For Jantzen, this primary dualism of God/World (creation *ex nihilo*)

was itself constructed as a theological justification for patriarchy. The dominant group of ruling class males constructed a world-view which set them apart as normative humanity, over against the "other" — women, other races, the poor, the earth — and then fashioned in their own image a God of ultimate value, power, and rationality over against the disvalue, passivity and irrationality of the opposite side of the duality.[48]

We pay a high price for this dualism, going as it does against the reality that we are all parts of the universe, for it creates "an unbridgeable chasm not just between us and the rest of the universe, but within our very selves."[49] This cosmic dualism is being played out in our own times in the fundamentalistic moral stance, which sees that the only way to resolve the tensions created by it is by literally destroying the world.[50]

As well as on the cosmic order, this Christian religious dualism is seen in Christian history. Here it appears, for example, as a conflict between the patriarchal order of creation and the egalitarian order of redemption. In this dualistic way of thinking, the patriarchal order of creation is the order that applies to both church and state, with equivalence reserved for heaven. On the other hand, the egalitarian order of redemption applies to a small church minority only, a minority usually associated with celibacy and prophecy such as is found in the Shaker community. This Christian historical dualism was broken by the Enlightenment, which severed the connection between patriarchalism and the theology of creation. In its place was posited a theology of creation based on an understanding of all humans as being in the imago Dei. Thus all Christians were freed to establish the just social order rather than waiting for heaven.[51] In an ecofeminist perspective, this egalitarian community would include not only the human but the non-human.

This dualistic posture in Christian history can be seen not only in the understanding of creation and redemption, but also in the view of the female-male relationship. Throughout its history, the dominant and official view has been that of a theology of subordination, a theology

> based on the notion of male headship of the order of creation. This notion basically identifies patriarchal social order with the natural or divinely created order. Male headship is thus regarded as rooted in the intrinsic nature of things and willed by God. Any effort to upset this order by giving women autonomy or equal rights would constitute a rebellion against God and would result in moral and social chaos in human society. This notion that male headship is the order of creation usually carries with it the hidden or explicit assumption that God is male or at least properly represented by symbols of paternal authority.[52]

This view of male headship carries with it an understanding of women as the moral, ontological, and intellectual inferiors of men. "Her subordination is not merely one of social office, but of actual inferiority."[53] (The minority view of a theology of equivalence will be examined in the next section under the issue of complementarity.)

It may be argued that this theology of subordination is not true to its Christian roots; one sees evidence for a different understanding of women as evidenced by the writings of the Christian scriptures.[54] Our model for

Christian dualism may in fact come out of ancient Greek philosophy. Ruether looks back to the Greek philosophers and notes:

> For Plato, the resistance of the primal matrix to formation by infinite ideals is regarded as the intrinsically evil character of "matter," which indicates its inferior moral and ontological nature. Women are the primary symbols of this lower moral and ontological sphere which is to be repressed and subjugated. In social terms this means that women are cut out of the "progress" of male civilization. They are forbidden to participate in the formation of its sanctioning religious, education, and political processes. While males use knowledge to free themselves from biological determination, women are subjugated all the more to exclusively biological processes. They are forbidden knowledge and control of the technology that would place their own biological processes in their own hands (contraception, abortion, gynecology). Thus the structures of patriarchal consciousness that destroy the harmony of nature are expressed symbolically and socially in the repression of women.[55]

As well as in Christian history and in Greek philosophy, the female/male dualism is seen in the lives of third-world women; their work, done in cooperation with nature's processes and for purposes of sustenance and to satisfy needs, is devalued in general. They suffer more and more from real poverty while the masculinist model continues to speak of the need to raise the incomes of the poor and to invest in new technologies. This is coupled with the illusion that more income and more technology could alleviate the environmental crisis![56]

This male/female dualism is also modeled in our social roles:

> Women are trained for private virtue, men for public power; and the severance between the sexes and the two realms is responsible for much of our irrational thinking and behavior. ... *To disconnect virtue from power is to ensure that virtue will be powerless, and licenses power to be without virtue.* Those who closet themselves in a fugitive and cloistered virtue must remain adamantly ignorant or confess themselves participants in evil; those who stand only in the world and never gaze at the inner life, at connections among people, at the sharing and bonding that make all life possible, stride off and become the evil.[57]

This same dualism of private virtue *vs.* public power may be seen behind the thinking which is trying to place the burden for the ecological crisis on the private sector. However, since ecological immorality is grounded basically in the patterns of production and social exploitation, any changes made in the private sector can only be tokenism.[58] Rather, what is needed is to bring the virtuous people into the public domain and to make the public domain a place where morality is a reality.

While the above examples of dualism—God *vs.* the World; creation *vs.* redemption; male *vs.* female; public *vs.* private—can be seen as creating a context which is conflictual, at least one writer would argue that dualism can exist in a situation where neither side is independent of or better than the other. Barbara A. Reed calls this "complementary dualism" and cites terms such as *yin and yang, male and female, wind and rain, summer and winter.*[59] It is to this issue of complementary dualism or complementarity that we now turn, possibly to shed light on solutions to the problems that have been raised through an analysis of instrumentalism and dualism.

Complementarity

Through human ways of thinking as well as in the forces of nature itself, there is evidence of opposites being held together in a delicate balance. It would seem that if this balance is not maintained, the whole system, as well as its parts, suffers. In this section, I will cite several examples of this balancing or complementary dualism in both the secular and the religious worlds and look at some of the issues that a theory of complementarity includes, such as transcendence and the place of complementarity in the context of our contemporary world-view.

On the cosmic level, the forces of yin and yang are seen as complementary, with yang understood as representing that which is active, male, light, positive, heaven, life, and so forth, and yin understood as representing that which is passive, female, dark, negative, Earth, death, and so on.[60] This same model of balance forms the basis for the contemporary theory of chaos. This theory is based on the interplay of forces on the atomic scale and forces on the everyday scale; its essence is seen in the delicate balance between the forces of stability and the forces of instability.[61] This may be nature's way of telling us that it is both order and creativity that form the basis for life. On a more mundane level, the same model of balance may be seen in the markings of my cat, Russell. The orange and white patternings on either side of his body are thoroughly dissimilar, yet together, mysteriously, they form a balanced whole; they hold creativity and order in a delicate and beautiful balance.

This model of balance is also operative in the religious sphere. For example, it seems to be the model used by Rosemary Ruether for what she calls a theology of equivalence. She sees this theology as the minority view of the female/male relationship. As was the majority view of a theology of subordination, which was discussed in the section entitled "Dualism," this minority view has also been present throughout Christian history. A theology of equivalence is open to the possibility of differences but interprets these differences in a non-hierarchical manner. The scriptural texts on which this theology is based are Genesis 1:27; Galatians 3:28; and Acts 2:17.[62]

A theology which is open to a possibility of differences could also be employed regarding such issues as personal immortality (in which men seem to have a greater interest than do women); redemption (is it a masculine understanding, involving a need to be freed from sin or a feminine understanding, involving a need for creativity?); and sin (often seen by women in terms of self-abnegation and by men in terms of pride). It could also be used to enhance our understanding of a Divinity who is both female and male. While the possibilities for theologizing are very rich here, there are at least two issues of concern. The first is our ability (or lack thereof) to hold two different views simultaneously. The way out might be to opt for transcendence so that, in fact, we would not have to deal with the tensions involved with holding the differences simultaneously. This is the model used by, for example, Carol Ochs, who understands the Divinity as neither father nor mother nor parent, but rather as the ordering principle of the world.[63] On the positive side, this would enable us to see transcendence, not as other, but as a term applied to a Divinity who is more than a sum of parts.[64] On the negative side, we would find ourselves, as does Ochs, in a position of theistic monism—a position some of us would find untenable.

A second problem is this: Can one legitimately situate a theory/practice of complementarity within a world-view in which the reality is "the asymmetry of male dominance."[65] What, in fact, does complementarity mean in a setting which is, by definition, unbalanced? As long as our way of living is competitive rather than cooperative and our god is the free market economy, the theory/practice of complementarity is an anomaly. For a theory/practice of complementarity to become a reality, we would have to hold a world-view where differences are truly honored (McDonald's in Tokyo!). But it is not only the differences that must be honored; there must also be a sense of unity. It is to this issue of diversity and unity, the many and the one, the particular and the universal, that we now turn.

The One and the Many

As with any valid philosophical category, that of the one and the many will manifest itself in a broad spectrum of areas. In this section, I will limit my examples to a few areas that are particularly pertinent to the concerns of this book. Examples include the replacement of the matricentric cultures by patriarchy; the disciplines of history and theology; and world religions. Last, we will examine this issue of unity and diversity to see what light it can shed on our understanding of the human person.

The economist Hazel Henderson sees the overthrow of the matrifocal cultures by patriarchy as rooted in biology. According to Henderson, in matrifocal cultures, the genotype (the species as a whole) not the phenotype (the individual) was the core component. The Goddess/Mother/Earth was the primary metaphor. The core value system of the genotype could be found

> in its celebration of the processes of life, its changes, cycles, seasons, subtle forces, as well as the positive value of decay, entropy and death, all of which allows the grand experiment of evolution to unfold. Phenotypes must die if each new generation is to have its chance. But the dying of the body on the material plane of existence is also one more transition, if we have a larger view of ourselves as an integral part of creation: temporarily constituted as a sensory cell of the body of Gaia, but also having a transcendent dimension, as all our spiritual traditions describe. I believe that the early patriarchal revolt against the societies which worshipped the Mother Goddess was partly the agonized scream of the phenotype's newly-individuated, ego-awareness rebelling against the great implacable Goddess/Mother/Earth: the genotype's metaphors for the genotype, that decreed the phenotype's sacrifice and death-sentence. If there is any substance to this hypothesis, it may explain the deeply-buried fear of women, mother and earth and their mythic connection with decay, entropy and death, expressed in mythology and recently examined in male psychology.[66]

We are now at a point in history where we can see the consequences of an overemphasis on the individual: in the homeless that wander our streets; in the species whose lives are forever gone so that some humans may have more than enough; in the destruction of the water and air which belong to our children's children. Even if we were able, which we are not, the answer would not lie in a return to a matricentric society. Rather, we must develop a world that recognizes not only the individual—the individual in other species, as well as the human—but also the fact that all are united in that all are a part of one Earth. This new age would be neither matricentric nor patriarchal, but rather omnicentric—a true honoring of unity and diversity in all of the Creation.[67]

This same principle of unity and diversity can be employed in disciplines as disparate as history and theology. In doing history, Carolyn Merchant employs what she calls an ecosystem model. In this model, history is seen from the ground up, with the natural and human factors both forming an interdependent system. Further, nature and culture are viewed, not in a dualistic fashion, but as components in a dynamically interactive system.[68]

David Tracy comments on this same issue of the one and the many in light of the contribution that he sees being made by feminist theology. For Tracy, the contexuality-universality issue is particularly exemplified in feminist theology: the context via the material realities of gender, sex, class, and race, and the universality in the non-negotiable ethical commitment to justice and equality on gender issues.[69] He calls feminist theology "that at once most contextual and most universally ethical form of theology in our period."[70] He goes on to note that to let go of either contextuality or universality would plunge feminist theology (all theology) into "self-contradiction, indeed self-destruction."[71]

This same holding in tension of unity and diversity may be seen in some of the world religions, especially in terms of image and symbol. For Hinduism, it may be argued that its very unity lies in its ability to embrace diversity. Diana Eck goes on to note that "India's affirmation of Oneness is made in a context that affirms with equal vehemence the multitude of ways in which human beings have seen that Oneness and expressed their vision."[72]

In Christianity, the primary symbol is one of unity and multiplicity—that of the Christian Trinity. And within that symbol itself, there seems to be justification in looking upon the Holy Spirit as the universal aspect of salvation, while Jesus, as a special manifestation of the Word, symbolizes salvation for a particular group of people.[73] Jantzen, in perceiving the world as the very body of the Divinity, also holds for maintaining this balance between the one and the many. The unity is there because reality is one; nothing exists outside of the Divinity.[74] But the many are also there because creative love, that is, God, "gives autonomy to that which it creates."[75] The mystical experience can also hold this tension in that it can be simultaneously an experience of unity and of the distinction between creature and Creator.[76]

The above examples look to the macrocosm to explicate the one and the many. We will now examine the microcosm—the human self—to see how this principle is played out.

For the philosopher Val Plumwood, the issue involved in developing an adequate account of the self is how to "stress continuity without drowning in a sea of indistinguishability."[77] She attempts to maintain this balanced tension by developing the concept of the relational self—a self that is distinct but also in continuity with the other. For this self-in-relationship, the relationships are essential, not accidental; they define what, in fact, it means to be human. This relational self avoids both the masculine separation accounts of the self and the feminine merger accounts.[78] Rather, it is "embedded in a network of essential relationships with distinct others."[79] Included with these distinct others are the members of the natural world with whom we recognize our continuity while also recognizing their independence and distinctness from us and the fact that their needs are different from ours.[80]

In summary, it may be said that ecofeminism is calling us to a new theology of nature, one that rethinks the whole idea that there is an ontological chain of being. In this new theology, spirit and matter are to be seen as the inside and outside of being. Ultimately, matter itself dissolves into energy, with energy providing the basis for what we experience as visible. The place where matter is most intensely organized—the cortex of the human brain and the central nervous system — is the site of the origin of human consciousness. This human consciousness allows us to respond as an I to the Thou which exists in every form of creation. This consciousness also make us aware that, while the less complex forms of life can exist perfectly without us, we are dependent for our very existence on them. This gift of intelligence today makes us aware that we have one of two options: to use our intelligence as servants in caring for and transforming the ecological community; or to destroy our own, and most others, life support systems through our continued destruction of the Earth. Today we are being called to a new form of human intelligence which is non-dualistic and Earth-centered. As contrasted to the outmoded forms of linear thinking, the new ecological thinking is diffuse and relational and takes into account the whole rather than merely some parts. The new ecological ethic recognizes the interconnection between the domination of certain groups of humans and the domination of nature. It calls for the working together of the nonhuman and the human as friends in the work of forming a new Creation.[81]

PART 2

THE EARTH

3.

Living the Earth-Centered Future Today

Many of us recognize that we have entered a new time in the story of our home, the Earth, and although we humans have shared her story only briefly, she seems to be counting on us to live lives which are in harmony with her rhythms and which celebrate her beauty. It is to be hoped that the decade of the 1990s will be noted by future generations as the time when a critical mass of people began living in a way that was truly Earth-centered; that the focus of our existence was our relationship to the Earth and all of its life forms.[1] This Earth-centered future must have its basis in both the theoretical, where issues such as values and an Earth-centered ethics are needed, and in the practical, where we need to address issues such as the meaning of the human and of our living in place (bioregionalism and Green politics). It is to these issues that this chapter is devoted in the spirit so well articulated by Lester Brown, who reminds us that "saving the planet is not a spectator sport."[2]

Values

We live in a time when the whole Earth community has been exposed to a single origin story.[3] The reaction to this story on the part of the scientific community and the religious community has implications for the issue of values. On the one hand, this origin story has been accepted by the scientific community which has, at the same time, rejected religious values. On the other hand, the religious community has placed emphasis on redemption and the next world and generally ignores the natural world. The result is that neither community—scientific or religious—has come to terms with the need to see value(s) in this world. But the reality is that both the physical/material and the psychic/spiritual are needed, as it is from these two dimensions that human consciousness emerges.[4] And as any parent or teacher knows only too well, we all come out of a value system, as do our

43

children. The real concern is: what are the values out of which we are living today?

With the collapse of the Soviet world, it is being claimed by some segments of society that we can now live as one World reaping the benefits of a capitalist system. That would leave us all "free" to enjoy the dominant values of capitalism such as individualism, competitiveness, domination, and consumption.[5] This may be summed up as a "morality" of power over (control). It was played out in the sands of Iraq, where we demonstrated our willingness to sacrifice countless innocent lives, including those of our own children, rather than consider a lessening of our ability to consume a dwindling energy source.[6] How often does the media speak in terms that recognize the finitude of the Earth's resources? When was the last time an ad was presented that spoke of all as deserving the necessities of life rather than of "me" as deserving more? Why are our children taught that history is the story of conquest and power over rather than the story of the good that has been done? Why is the murderous conquest of one man considered noteworthy and not an aberration?[7] One could continue this questioning, looking at all of our contemporary institutions, but I suspect that it is enough if we just pause in our everyday frenzy. That pause reveals to us that there is more to the human than being a consumer of the Earth's resources—a consumption that ultimately gives little satisfaction but does surely add more rubble to tomorrow's landfill. In stopping to listen to the voices inside ourselves, we might also listen to the voices of the Earth, for those voices speak to us of the values that are needed for life in the twenty-first century.

It seems that not only is the Earth capable of being a teacher of values, but also that there are some humans who have the ability to help us get in touch with her teaching. For example, the Sioux councils of governance included not only the standing people but also the swimming people, the creeping people, the flying people. And these people were to be heard, not only in the decision making processes of some Native American tribes, but in their celebrations as well. In the dances of the Pueblo—the deer dance, or the corn maiden dance, or the squash blossom dance—one encounters deer or corn or squash blossom speaking through the human. It may be said that these humans have been, as it were, seized by the spirit of these other life forms.[8] Nor is it impossible for those of us who are not part of the Native American culture to touch and be touched by other life forms. What is required is that we enter into a quiet space and invite the material form which wishes to speak through us to identify itself. What we have heard may then be shared in the Council of All Beings. Thus, for example, we can learn from a lichen, who works with time, the gift of patience.[9] The possibilities are endless.[10] Nor need this process be limited to group activities. In our own time Dian Fossey was able to share in an almost intimate fashion in the life of the gorilla community. How successful we will be in hearing the "other" speak depends in part on our understanding of language and the answers given to such questions as these: Is language only one type of a sign system? Is volition necessary for one to be considered a speaking subject? How effective is the "speaking" of those who do not use human language?[11] To these questions of Patrick Murphy, I add the following: How effective are we at hearing the voices of the "other"? How effective are we at "speaking" with other life forms?

If we do develop the capacities needed to learn from the Earth, there is much that we can be taught. These values could include mutualism, freedom, subjectivity, self-organization, the equality of non-equals, unity in diversity, non-hierarchical relationships, and spontaneity.[12] Each of us could add our own observations to those of Bookchin; these might include grace, beauty, awe, sexuality, and sustainability. While our understanding of each of these values, and many others, needs to be developed, the purposes of this writing should be served if we look at a value — that of sustainability — which speaks to ecologists from many spectrums.

Sustainability may be defined as "providing for ourselves in such a way that we don't reduce the ability of future generations to provide for themselves."[13] Activities which are non-sustainable include those which "lead to the extinction of other life forms" and those which "require resources in quantities that could never be available for all people."[14] For the ecofeminist Charlene Spretnak, the sustainability of a human system is grounded in the reality of its interrelatedness.[15]

While the issue of sustainability is ultimately global, the place to begin is in our own neighborhood. It is in the local setting that sustainability's goals of restoring natural systems, satisfying basic human needs, and developing support for individuals can begin to be met.[16]

We can begin in our own hearts by asking ourselves questions about the meaning of true riches. For it is not true that more is always better. As Francis Moore Lappé asks in regard to beef: For whom is more beef better? Not for the consumer, who suffers more heart attacks; not for the atmosphere, which receives more methane gases; not for the forests, which are destroyed by grazing cattle; not for the creatures who once were alive in the forests.[17] The Earth seems to be calling humans to the recognition that enough is plenty and that true affluence is spiritual rather than material.[18] Or, as Gary Snyder, the poet, puts it: "True affluence is not needing anything."[19] Nor is this just the dream of poets and mystics. A study done in the USA in the 1980s showed that fifteen million people "are basing their lives fully or partially on such values as frugality, human scale, self-determination, ecological awareness, and personal growth."[20] What is now the lived reality of a few must become the new value system of all. If we all learn to look to the Earth as our teacher, out of the value system that she teaches to the Earth community, we could develop an environmental ethics for the twenty-first century. It is to the issue of an environmental ethics, based on values rather than beliefs, that we now turn.

An Ethic of Care

The predominant ethic of our eroding patriarchal structure may be characterized as an ethic of domination: whether it is the domination of the male over the female and/or the domination of the human over nature. While this domination is sometimes presented in paternalistic terms, this does not negate the fact that, at its base, there lies an ethic of domination. Thus, for instance, on what basis can we claim the right to be nature's caretaker when the reality is that nature takes as good as or, in most cases, better care of itself without our help?[21] This ethic of domination is summed up in the words of Judith Plant, who states:

Hierarchy destroys. Based on power-over, it has no capacity for compassion. Given the hierarchical requisite to take in order to gain, it cannot empathize with people's needs and feelings. Rather, there are rules, tenets, within which we must mold ourselves to fit—thus destroying so much of our human need to create. How, and on what basis can we move away from these death-dealing ways?[22]

The move away from our "death-dealing ways" may be emerging in an environmental ethic capable of incorporating feminism. Karen J. Warren bases the need for environmental ethics to embrace feminism on three arguments. The first is the need for historical accuracy, which "requires acknowledging the historical feminization of nature and naturalization of women as part of the exploitation of nature."[23] The second is the need to achieve a conceptually adequate environmental ethics, which requires the realization that the domination of women and the domination of nature are twin dominations grounded in the Western "patriarchal conceptual framework characterized by a logic of domination."[24] The third is the need to clarify "how the domination of nature is conceptually linked to patriarchy and, hence, how the liberation of nature is conceptually linked to the termination of patriarchy."[25] Warren further notes that, without the word *feminist*, one is led to assume that environmental ethics has no bias whereas in fact it has a male-gender bias.[26] She argues out of an understanding, which she calls ecological feminism, grounded in historical, symbolic, and theoretical connections which exist between the domination of nonhuman nature and the domination of women.[27] This logic of domination must be replaced by a meaningful notion of difference.[28] That "meaningful notion of difference" is expressed by Carol P. Christ in the following words:

There are no hierarchies among beings on Earth. Yes, we are different from the swallows that fly, from the many-faceted stones on the beach, from the redwood trees in the forest. We may have more capacity to shape our lives than other beings, but you and I will never fly with the grace of a swallow, live as long as a redwood tree, nor endure the endless tossing of the sea like a stone. Each being has its own intrinsic beauty and value.[29]

While Christ celebrates the intrinsic value of the Earth itself, there are other strands of ecofeminism that look upon the Earth/human relationship in different terms. Three philosophical strands within ecofeminism are recognizable: one that recognizes the intrinsic value of the Earth itself as well as of all its creatures, including rivers, forests, and so on; in this human-Earth relationship, the Earth is considered sacred. A second strand of ecofeminism recognizes that human survival is dependent on the survival of the Earth itself. Third is the approach of indigenous people, which recognizes both the first and the second approaches. By recognizing both the intrinsic value of the Earth and our dependence on it for survival, the intent is to respect both our needs and those of the Earth.[30] An exclusive emphasis on the first approach could lead to an over-reliance on the Earth as sacred and her ability to right the wrongs of her children, no matter what their deeds. On the other hand, the second approach appears highly anthropo-centric, which speaks more to the problem than to its solution. Is not being used as a resource the reality of the degradation that both women and the Earth are currently experiencing?[31] It may at times be necessary to appeal to our human survival instincts. Gary Snyder does this when he warns us that, as we destroy the gene pool, we lessen our own chances for survival in that we destroy our ability to adapt and respond to new situations.[32] Or it may be necessary to appeal to our need for the aesthetic, as does Thomas Berry when he speaks of his fear that the coming environmental degradation will be such that we as a species will pray for extinction.[33] The issue rests in our holding in balance our needs and those of the other life forms. The third option—that of the human and the nonhuman as being here for one another—appears to be our most likely path to a future. Some ecofeminists are attempting to articulate this option through an environmental ethics of care.

Deane Curtin argues cogently for a politicized ecofeminist ethics of care based on the following principles. It would undercut the distinction between the public and the private arenas—something to which most, possibly all, ecofeminists would agree.

Second, an ethic of care needs to be contextualized but not privatized. In other words, it would involve caring for particular others in the contexts of their histories.[34] The insight of Marti Kheel of the need to identify with the particular is pertinent to this second criterion.[35] Elise Boulding also raises this issue when she speaks of the ability of the human—women and men—to become dehumanized when dealing in "larger perspectives and large-scale scanning skills."[36] Curtin's second criterion seems to take into account this need to particularize, but since he also stresses the wider context, he seems to be arguing against making the individual situation a world unto itself.

Third, Curtin postulates that an ethic of care involves the recognition that reciprocity may not be involved. He sights as examples those who are geographically remote or those who are of another species.[37] Our ability to care for another species, may rest, according to Patrick Murphy, on our ability to enter into dialogue; that is, our willingness to hear and actually be changed by the other.[38] This, in turn, rests on our willingness to recognize "a speaker/author who is not the speaking subject but a renderer of the 'other' as speaking subject."[39] It also rests on our ability to recognize human language as merely one form in a vast system of symbolic communication.[40]

> The point is not to speak for nature but to work to render the sig-nification presented us by nature into a verbal [?] depiction by means of speaking subjects, whether this is through characterization in the arts or through discursive prose. The test for whether such depictions seem accurate renderings of the speaking subjects will be the actions in the world that they call upon humans to perform.[41]

Murphy recognizes that there are always two voices present in these renderings. However, that recognition does not negate our need to struggle for such renderings—whether it is I for the mountain or men for the feminist theory.[42]

At least two further considerations raised by Roger J. H. King, may be mentioned as necessary if one is to develop an ethics of care. First is the concern that it may rely too heavily on individual lived experience or narrative. By what criteria is the narrative judged?[43] Jim Cheney's writing offers an interesting response to this concern through the suggestion that the narrative be grounded in geography. If one grounds the narrative in the self alone, it may be argued that this would lead to schizophrenia; if one grounds the narrative in the human alone, this would lead to the oppression of unity. A healthier response, for all concerned, is that the narrative be grounded in the Earth as nurturer and teacher.[44]

The second concern is the meaning given to the term *care*. King asks, for example, how a rock benefits from our caring? While he stresses that he is not looking for reciprocity, he does think that an ethics of care calls for a way in which the rock may be said to benefit. His solution lies in his making the issue moral rather than aesthetic.[45] This leaves him open to being able to see an ethics of care as offering

> the possibility that by refusing to draw arbitrary lines between human and non-human, a space can be held open in which the imagination may at least be educated to "loving perception" of the non-human world as a member of the moral community of difference and an object of care.[46]

The issue then becomes, How does the human become educated to this "loving perception"; in other words, the issue of transformation?

Transformation

Various descriptions have been offered concerning the present Earth crisis by persons both outside and inside the religious community. What the following descriptions have in common is the authors' perceptions that we are in crisis and that nothing short of a total transformation of our society is called for. Marilyn French, from a feminist perspective, sees us as a society without vision because we are a society without morality, that is, without values, without priorities.[47] Eli Sagan uses the model of the psyche to trace society's development into tyranny.[48] Quaker Paul Shannon sees the U.S.A. as operating out of a single center of power over, at the heart of which are the business, political, and military elites who originate our foreign and military policies.[49] Geologian Thomas Berry describes us as entranced with the industrially-driven consumer society.[50] The woman and the man "on the street" are more and more indicating their understanding that things are not right.

The analyses of our current crisis are many and varied; so are the methods of transformation. Given the concerns of this book, we will limit ourselves to looking at transformation from an Earth-centered perspective. From that viewpoint, it seems that the Earth has entered into a new kind of relationship with humankind. Berry describes this relationship in the following words:

> The earth that directed itself instinctively in its former phases seems now to be entering a phase of conscious decision through its human expression. This is the ultimate daring venture for the earth, this confiding its destiny to human decision, the bestowal upon the human community of the power of life and death over its basic life systems.[51]

If Berry is correct in his assessment of the human/Earth relationship, the task before us is enormous. Where might we begin?

Those of us who formed the Center for Women, the Earth, the Divine (C:WED) found ourselves one day without further energy for entering the task of transformation This changed when we shared the following paragraphs by Julia Scofield Russell:

> As we transform ourselves, we transform our world. Not later. Now. Simultaneously. How can this be so? The practice of the politics of lifestyle springs from an understanding of how things actually happen rather than the linear, cause-and-effect model. As we align ourselves with the regenerative powers of the Earth and the evolutionary thrust

of our species, we tap abilities beyond the ordinary. We move into the Tao.

How do you initiate this process in your life? You can start just about anywhere. You can start with recycling, with your means of transportation, with your diet and food-buying practices, with composting, with your relationships, with meditation, tax resistance, right livelihood, housing, gardening, conversation—it's up to you. What seems easiest, most obvious, or most urgent to you? Start there.[52]

What we learned is that we had in fact already seriously begun the work—and play—of transformation, but each in a different way: though parenting, through politics, through spirituality, through an Earth-conscious diet, through study. What we have in common is our motivation: our desire to heal the Earth that we love.

This issue of motivation is critical if transformation is to become a reality, for if we do the right things for the wrong reasons, nothing will change. This is made very explicit by Bookchin:

> To reenter natural evolution merely to rescue our hides from ecological catastrophe would change little, if anything, in our sensibilities and institutions. Nature would still be object (only this time to be feared rather than revered), and people would still be objects instrumentally oriented toward the world (only this time cowed rather than arrogant). . . . Only the most spontaneous desire to be natural—that is, to be fecund, creative and intrinsically human, can now justify our very *right* to reenter natural evolution as conscious social beings.[53]

Once we have reentered the web of life and done so for the right reasons, we are confronted with the reality that our cultural traditions are the major source of our current problems. This being the case it appears that we need to move beyond our cultural traditions to our genetic coding to ask for guidance.[54] "We do invent our cultural coding, but the power to do so is itself consequent on the imperatives of our genetic coding."[55] It is our genetic coding which provides the basic physical and psychic structure of our being.[56] In tapping our genetic coding, we tap millions of years of human evolution.

Beyond our genetic coding we need to go to the Earth itself and the Universe itself: the Earth because it is our source and carries the physical form and psychic structure of all the Earth's beings; the Universe because it has the capacity for intelligible order and is the source of all creative energy. We ourselves are a dimension of the Universe. Any authenticity we have is derived from the spontaneities within ourselves, the Earth, the Universe.[57] In summary, it may be said that the ultimate custody of the Earth belongs to the Earth itself. It is the role of the human to listen and learn from what she is telling us.[58]

One possible model in organizing for transformation is the organic model of a tree. At the heart of the tree would be the elements of earth (North), air (East), fire (South), and water (West).[59] As one example, the Earth issues include pesticides, preservation of sacred lands, and feeding the hungry.[60] In this organic model, it is recognized that

> environmental issues are social justice issues, for it is the poor who are forced to work directly with unsafe chemicals, in whose neighborhoods toxic waste incinerators are planned, who cannot afford to buy bottled water and organic vegetables or pay for medical care. Environmental issues are international issues for we cannot simply export unsafe pesticides, toxic wastes and destructive technologies without poisoning the whole living body of the Earth. And environmental issues are women's issues, for women sicken, starve and die from toxics, droughts, and famines, their capacity to bear new life is threatened by pollution, and they bear the brunt of care for the sick and the dying, as well as for the next generation.[61]

We must understand the connections between issues; otherwise, we adopt false solutions. Rounding out the organic model, the roots of the tree symbolize the economy, as seen in terms of economic democracy as well as political democracy and an economy that is sustainable. The heart of the tree symbolizes our treatment of one another based on the recognition that all have inherent value. In summary, the implementation of this organic model depends on our forming small communities based on commitment to one another and to political and spiritual work for the long term.[62]

Instead of using the word *transformation*, Marilyn French speaks in terms of a moral revolution. She sees the current moral revolution—the feminist movement—as basically different from any preceding revolution in that it is the first revolution that involves protesting patriarchy itself.[63] She argues:

> Only a fundamental moral revolution can provide what is needed for real change in human institutions and behavior. This too many thinkers have attempted to supply. But they all encounter a basic stumbling block: to get to the meaning of power as a value, and to get it into a more realistic perspective, it is necessary to reexamine the traditional relations between men and women, the traditional notion of the female and her association with nature, and to confront the fact that the entire establishment of patriarchy is founded on the ambition to usurp the natural position of women. Male thinkers have been unwilling or unable to do this.[64]

Eleanor Haney also talks in terms of revolution and of the specifically feminist virtue that is needed today. For Haney, this virtue has three components. The first is *competence*, where the unique being of each is used for the self and for others. The second is *vulnerability*, which involves the willingness to be a risk-taker—the willingness to be open to change and to be changed. Together competence and vulnerability enable one to grow in power and integrity. The third element of feminist virtue is *passionate constancy*, which involves the coming together of steadfastness and commitment with love, anger, and intense energy. When brought together, anger, and love can both feed and ground one another.[65]

While the above paragraphs offer at least a beginning understanding of what is involved if we are truly to change the world, it is appropriate that we remind ourselves of our unity, that all is a part of nature. This unity can be experienced in our understanding of all on Earth and the Earth itself as primarily recycled star dust. In reality, it is the material of our bodies that is immortal; at death, only the form changes.[66]

As a concrete sign of our entering into transformation, it might be well to look around and make a covenant with one other creature—not a human—with whom one is willing to develop a special relationship.[67] This could be a particular brook, or hill, or companion animal or ... This covenant validates in a special way two different life forms—and their connectedness—in the web of life. Making the covenant with one who is close by enhances our understanding of being part of a particular place. It is to this issue of understanding and living in a particular place, or bioregionalism, that we now turn.

Bioregionalism

We begin this section by looking at the relationship between ecofeminism and bioregionalism. An attempt will then be made to define bioregionalism, to amplify this definition through description, and to observe the gathering of bioregionalists.

For some ecofeminists, the relationship between ecofeminism and bioregionalism is specifically stated. For Plant, bioregionalism is seen as the way to implement the philosophy of ecofeminism in a practical way. It is the way for an ecofeminist to live out what is being thought.[68] For Cheney, "bioregionalism is a natural extension of the line of thought being developed by those advocating a view of ethics as contextualist and narrative."[69] According to Marnie Muller, bioregionalism challenges hierarchical thinking, which she sees as encapsulated in the male god's dominion over heaven and the human male's dominion over all of its inhabitants—human and nonhuman. Bioregionalism also challenges body/mind dualism and brings us back to a reality which is sensual, which allows us to experience the creation through all of our senses. It also challenges our seeing home as the place to get away from and resacralizes it—both the immediate home which shelters us and our home, the Earth.[70]

Other ecofeminists do not explicitly cite the connection between ecofeminism and bioregionalism, but their writing seems to validate this connection. Thus, for example, Val Plumwood argues for the need to be related to particular places, animals, and so forth. She looks to the indigenous peoples as a model for establishing these relationships.[71] While in no way negating this model, I suggest that the bioregional movement could also serve, for her purposes of relatedness to the particular, as a model. And Indian ecofeminist Shiva speaks of women and tribal peoples who are having their basic needs met through healthy local foods, houses constructed of local materials, and clothing made of natural fibers.[72] The lifestyles of these women and tribal people, and the lifestyles advocated by the bioregionalists, have much in common although the third-world and first-world differences will not be easy to overcome.

How, then, might one define a bioregion? Succinctly, a *bioregion* is "an identifiable geographical area of interacting life systems that is relatively self-sustaining in the ever-renewing process of nature."[73] Bioregions provide primary biological identity rather than an identity which is ethnic or political or social.[74] In other words, a bioregion is a total life community whose functions are carried out by all the members of the community.[75] These functions may be defined as follows: self-propagating; self-nourishing; self-educating; self-governing; self-healing; self-fulfilling. The key to understanding these functions is that they are not centered on the human but on all the members of the community.[76] Thus, for example, the primary example of self-education is the Earth itself, which "has performed unnumbered billions of experiments in designing the existing life system."[77]

As well as being "relatively self-sustaining," the bioregions are all interdependent. This is seen in an obvious manner through the air systems and the water systems which flow across the entire planet. Also, the movements of many birds and animals are not bound by bioregions. (Nor are those of the human.) In other words, the Earth itself is an interrelated system comprised of bioregions.[78]

Another bioregionalist, Jim Dodge, also begins by seeing the essence of bioregionalism as first found in a sense of place. However, Dodge's criteria for determining one's bioregion expand beyond the biological to include the cultural and spiritual. He sees the essence of bioregionalism as residing secondly in a sense of local decision-making. And third, he locates the essence of bioregionalism in its lived spirituality—a spirituality centered on the love of all life. Dodge equates the above with theory; for him, the practice of bioregionalism lives mainly in the two avenues of resistance and renewal.[79]

In *Dwellers in the Land*, Kirkpatrick Sale develops a bioregional model through contrast to the industrio-scientific model.[80] He applies this contrast to what he calls the "four basic determinants of any organized civilization: scale, economy, polity, and society."[81] In regard to scale, Sale argues that the bioregion provides us with the optimum scale, for it is "not so small as to be powerless and impoverished, not so large as to be ponderous and impervious."[82] Rather, it possesses a scale in which there is equilibrium between ecological reality and human potential. Reading Gaea's laws shows that the Earth is organized into natural regions, not artificial states. Most natural regions are smaller than our current nation-states. Large bioregions—for instance, the approximately forty on the North American continent—break down into smaller and sometimes yet smaller bioregions—rather like Chinese boxes. Sale calls these, starting with the largest, ecoregions, georegions, and morphoregions. There are strong indications that the Native Americans lived as bioregionalists. Thus, for example, the Algonkian-speaking peoples inhabited the ecoregion of the Northeast hardwoods, while the tribes within this conglomerate, such as the Pennacook, the Masschuset, the Montauk, and the Mahican inhabited georegions defined by bodies of water and land characteristics. In addition, subtribes and language subgroups inhabited smaller regions, which are comparable to morphoregions; for example, the Narragansets and the Wampanoag in the Narragansett Bay georegion.[83]

The second law we learn from Gaea in regard to scale is that of community. We see communities around us every day: flocks of birds, schools of fish, hills of ants, hives of bees.[84] Sale suggests that we may be the community that Gaea looks to for the "gathering, sorting, processing, storing, and using of information."[85]

Sale discusses the other determinants of the bioregional model: economy, polity, and society. Under economy, he raises the issues of conservation (as contrasted to the industrio-scientific element of exploitation); stability (as contrasted to change/progress); self-sufficiency *vs.* world economy; and cooperation *vs.* competition. Under polity he discusses decentralization (centralization); complementarity (hierarchy); and diversity (uniformity). Finally, under society the issues are symbiosis (polarization); evolution (growth/violence); and division (monoculture). The natural world is the model used to develop most of these elements.[86]

Sale not only offers the above model of bioregionalism, but he also offers very concrete suggestions on how one may respond to the Earth crisis, namely, by understanding the Earth as a living being (Gaea), a being who is in a real sense sacred and worthy of a response appropriate to her sacredness.[87] In practical terms, this is how Sale defines the essence of bioregionalism:

> But to become dwellers in the land, to relearn the laws of Gaea, to come to know the earth fully and honestly, the crucial and perhaps only and all-encompassing task is to understand place, the immediate specific place where we live. The kinds of soils and rocks under our feet; the source of the waters we drink; the meaning of the different kinds of winds; the common insects, birds, mammals, plants, and trees; the particular cycles of the seasons; the times to plant and harvest and forage—these are the things that are necessary to know. The

limits of its resources; the carrying capacities of its lands and waters; the places where it must not be stressed; the places where its bounties can best be developed; the treasures it holds and the treasures it withholds—these are the things that must be understood. And the cultures of the people, of the populations native to the land and of those who have grown up with it, the human social and economic arrangements shaped by and adapted to the geomorphic ones, both urban and rural settings—these are the things that must be appreciated.[88]

Sale is clear in his understanding that bioregionalism is not an utopian model, but rather a practical model that can become a reality because it contains these elements: its irrevocable grounding in historical realities; its accord with the present patterns of the industrial world; its vision of the future as real and practical and able to be realized without totally altering the present.[89] Others who argue for the practicality of bioregionalism include Bill Mollison, who contends that we have the ability to solve all of our problems—air, water, soil, money—and to do so locally;[90] and David Wheeler, who suggests we use bioregions as the given habitat areas for identifying human carrying capacity.[91]

But writing and reading about bioregionalism and those who connect it with the here and now does not necessarily put us in touch with those elements that strongly speak to living our Earth-centered future in the present. These can be experienced at a Bioregional Congress. Almost two years after the event (North American Bioregional Congress IV, August 1990, in the Gulf of Maine Bioregion), several strong impressions remain with me. These include a model where play was truly as important as work; the presence of those who spoke for other life forms such as spiders; the conviction that by utilizing the facilitation skills of someone like a Carolyn Estes, a large diverse group could effectively make decisions by consensus; the change of name from North America Bioregional Congress to Turtle Island Bioregional Congress to better reflect our native roots; the certainty that this was a movement begun and led by the Spirit.[92] How will bioregionalism develop in the future? Part of the answer to that question lies in its relationship to the Green movement.

The Green Movement

For historical purposes, it is worth noting that the initial formalizing of a Green organization in the United States of America took place at the North American Bioregional Congress I held in May of 1984 in the Ozark bioregion.[93] The natural connection between bioregionalism and a Green political model has been seen by those such as Sale who put the attainment of the bioregional model in terms of a political project.[94] But some bioregionalists express reservations about the Green movement. While seeing its value for the "short haul," Gene Marshall, for example, judges it ultimately not radical enough to effect the changes that are needed in response to our current crisis.[95] Also, Peter Berg cites basic differences between the bioregional movement and the Green party. For Berg, the Greens are generic in their goals, such as incorporating "ecological wisdom," while the bioregionalists are more specific; thus, for example, the bioregional goal of sustainability, which means restored natural habitats, meeting basic human needs, and supporting individuals in their life places.[96] By bringing definition to the Greens and their movement, our understanding of who they are and the relationship that exists between them and the bioregionalists should become more explicit. It is to that definition that we now turn our attention.

The Greens themselves use a slogan: "We are neither left nor right; we are in front." And, according to at least one study that has been done of the Green movement, the observation has been made that they do transcend the old political framework of left *vs.* right, for they are described as a movement which is ecological, holistic, and feminist.[97] For Charlene Spretnak and Fritjof Capra, the Greens are "the political manifestation of the cultural shift to the new paradigm."[98] At their core are the concepts of sustainability and interrelatedness, while Spretnak suggests that "human systems are sustainable to the extent that they reflect the fact of interrelatedness."[99]

On the international level, the first Green party was the Values Party in New Zealand, which was formed in the late 1960s. While it fell victim to internal bickering, it did serve as an inspiration through its 1975 election program, which included

> the need for a steady-state population and economy, new industrial and economic relations, ecological thinking, human-centered technology, soft-path energy systems, decentralization of government, equality for women, and rights of native peoples, as well as for valuing the traits traditionally considered feminine: cooperation, nurturing, healing, cherishing, and peace-making.[100]

It was almost halfway around the world and in the northern hemisphere, that the first Green party members were elected to a national parliament. This occurred in Belgium in 1981 with the election of members from two different Green parties.[101] However, the first time most North Americans heard about the Greens was in March of 1983 when twenty-seven members of the West German Parliament, representing the Green party, processed through the streets of Bonn carrying banners, flowers, and tree branches on their way to be seated for the opening parliamentary session. Their strength was based on their ties to the grassroots peace and ecology movements.[102] They symbolized a new kind of politics, "one in which human and ecological values outweigh the usual demands of power, and working for real peace begins by healing our relationship with the earth."[103]

Spretnak and Capra found in the West Germany Greens an understanding of the human as a part of nature. Also, as peace activists and ecologists, these Greens perceived the interconnection among the principles of ecological wisdom, a secure peace, a viable economy, and participatory grassroots democracy. (It was the lack of these principles in the existing parties that seems to have led, initially, to the formation of the West German Green party.) Initially, four principles appeared as part of the Green platform: ecology in terms of deep ecology; social responsibility, that is, social justice for minorities, poor, and women; grassroots democracy; and nonviolence.[104] In addition, many Greens advocate the principle of decentralization; they favor the recognition of regions (usually based on culture) rather than the present nonviable large nation-states.[105] Also, for some, the issue of feminist/postpatriarchal values forms a sixth principle.[106] An Earth-centered spirituality is a seventh principle articulated by many West German Greens (but not for some leftists who deny any spiritual principle). Included in this principle of an Earth-centered spirituality is the need for personal transformation.[107] Utilizing these principles and developing others was a work done by the Greens in the U.S.A. It is to the history of the Greens in that country that we now turn our attention.

Brian Tokar finds the origin for the Greens in North America in movements such as civil rights, student, peace, feminist, environmental, and antinuclear.[108] Moving deeper than the movements, he finds the inspiration for a Green vision to be based in observing the patterns found in the natural world. These patterns include the interconnectedness of all, unity-in-diversity, the fluidity of boundaries and social structures, and complementarity.[109]

Capra and Spretnak also contend that the vision already exists in the U.S.A. that would form the basis for a viable Green party. But while they see that vision coming out of the movements, as does Tokar, they see it even more in the holistic paradigm articulated in society and science. This holistic paradigm is becoming a lived reality through the political practices that are starting to emerge with, for example, the joining together of the feminist with the ecology and the peace movements.[110] From the West German Green experience, they see several lessons that can be learned. These include the need for a feminist critique on all major issues, not just that of sexism, and the need to make postpatriarchal values a lived reality.[111]

As well as the basis in the movements, an already articulated vision, and the lessons taught by the West German Greens, the U.S.A. Greens probably can profit from the frustration generated for many by recent presidential elections, as evidenced, for example, by the small number who voted. Spretnak and Capra describe this situation in the following terms:

> In this country a broad spectrum of people have grown frustrated with the sorry ritual we stage every four years, in which the Democrats and Republicans attack each other's performance, appeal with slick media

campaigns to our desires for a better society, and sell us old-paradigm solutions to our problems that are gravely ineffectual. Rather than a coherent program with a long term vision of sustainability and the quality of life, we are offered the marketing of a hero figure with his empty rhetoric and promises of short-term fixes.[112]

However, it would not be correct to see the Greens only in terms of being a political party. They may also be seen as a movement which employs oppositional tactics including community organizing, lobbying, nonviolent direct action, and reconstructive tactics such as the development of alternative technologies and raising bioregional awareness.[113] One method that is used to raise bioregional awareness — and to address any other issue that may be deemed important or necessary — is the Committees of Correspondence.[114] It was the Committees of Correspondence that were instrumental in helping to develop the ten key values of the U.S.A. Green movement. As well as the principles mentioned above in the discussion of the West German Greens (but excluding the principle on spirituality), these values are community-based economics, respect for diversity, global responsibility, and future focus.[115]

While the principle of an Earth-centered spirituality is not found among the Green key values, that should not lead one to conclude that spirituality is not important to many Greens and inherent in the other Green principles. Spretnak suggests that the spiritual dimension of Green politics must be compatible with its cultural dimension; that is, it must be posthumanist, postmodernist, and postpatriarchal. In a more concrete vein, she contends that Green spirituality must take into account the reality of religion in the U.S.A., that is, it must be pluralistic; it must resonate with the 69 percent of people who are affiliated with institutional religion; it must resonate with those who are affiliated with the Greens; it must inspire people to do their own thinking; it must be in harmony with key Green principles.[116] For Spretnak, spirituality seems to be grounded in an experience of unity as well as in an understanding of the mystical traditions and a growth process that leads to Wisdom.[117] Spretnak fleshes out her understanding of spirituality in terms of its meaning for the human person; the person's relationship to the environment; and the relationships among persons.[118] She sees the Green-orientated spiritual goals of spiritual development through inner growth, of ecological wisdom, of social responsibility, of gender equality as already part of our religious traditions.[119] In summary, it may be said that Green spirituality would be based on the deep ecology principles of interdependence, diversity, openness, and adaptability, and the spiritual principles of cultivating compassion and wisdom.[120]

It seems appropriate to conclude this chapter, which began with values and ended with politics, with a quote from Marilyn French, who states:

Morality is a personal and communal affair; when it reaches the public realm, it is called politics. The relation of the two is not like two sides of a coin, but like the inner and outer skins of the balloon; that is, it is the same thing, seen from inside or outside. Rousseau claimed that separating morality from politics made both disciplines incomprehensible. . . . Feminists say simply, the personal is the political.[121]

4.

Toward a Contemporary Cosmology

In just a few short centuries we have gone from an understanding of an Earth-centered Universe in which the human was viewed as the pinnacle of all visible creation to an understanding that the Earth is a minor planet in a minor solar system in a minor galaxy in a Universe filled with perhaps a hundred billion galaxies.[1] In such a Universe, the role of the human appears, at first glance, so insignificant as to not be worthy of mention. However, we are the ones who have been blessed with this knowledge of a Universe of incomprehensible beauty and creativity—the first creatures that we know of who are able to see in any detail our neighboring galaxies with their billions of stars—the first creatures who are able to contemplate, on a scientific basis, the beginning of the evolving Universe as it explodes as energy and time.

But this place of privilege which is the gift of modern science does not mean that we are the first to try to understand the nature of the Universe. In fact, in the Western world there has existed since the time of the Greek philosophers the science of cosmology, that "branch of philosophy that treats the origin and structure of the universe."[2] While the Greeks disagreed among themselves in regard to the particulars of cosmology, they largely shared an understanding of a Universe that "is limited in space, has neither a beginning nor end in time, is dominated by a set of unalterable laws, and has a definite and recurring rhythm."[3] It was the cosmologies of the Middle Ages that introduced the concepts of divine creation and annihilation, providence, and miracle.[4] In our own time, a cosmologist would ask such questions as Where did the universe come from? How and why did it begin? Will it come to an end, and if so, how?[5]

While the answers given by contemporary science to questions such as these form the content for the main part of this chapter, we also consider the contribution of myth and mysticism as well as input from Western theology to our story of the Universe.[6] Finally, we consider the role of the Christian Divinity in our new story of the Universe, a story given to us humans as we enter into the Earth Age.

Relating Myth, Mysticism, and Science

It is the function of myth to explain the origin of the Universe and the order of humankind. Within this function, mythic thinking is not characterized as accidental but rather as purposeful and reflective of an ideological structure.[7] It would be possible to make this same statement but with science as the subject rather than myth.

From a feminist perspective, it may be argued that there are two kinds of myths: social charter myths, which justify the present behavior of men toward women; and transforming myths, which present the female as evil by definition.[8] In this feminist perspective, it may be seen that the function of myth is once again purposeful and representative of a certain worldview. If we limit ourselves specifically to creation myths, in keeping with the content of this chapter, we find that matrilineal (in which descent is characterized as coming through the mother) societies retain feminine creation symbolism whereas patrilineal societies lack feminine creation symbolism.[9] French cites Joseph Campbell and his understanding of creation myths as evolving through four stages.[10] In the first state, the world is created by a goddess acting alone. Our oldest recorded creation myth speaks of the Sumerian deity Nammu, the Mother who gave birth to heaven and earth as well as all the deities and also decided that humans should be created.[11] In the second stage, the world is created by a goddess acting with a consort. An example is Gaea, the Earth, who alone created Heaven and mated with him to create the deities of the heavens.[12] In the third stage of the creation myths, the body of the goddess is used in some way by a male to create the world. Thus, for example, in the Babylonian epic of creation, *Enuma Elish*, the male god Marduk destroys the female goddess Tiamat, who was originally the creator of all.[13] In the fourth stage of the myths on creation, we find that the male god acts alone to create the world. This is the model used in the creation story found in the two accounts in Genesis.[14] If Campbell is correct in his exposition of the four stages found in the creation myths, we have graphic evidence of the use of myth to change and enforce the consciousness of a particular world-view at different times in the Earth's story.

In Asia, a different kind of creation story has proven itself to be a remarkable foreshadowing of modern science. In the *Purānas,* we read of the ages of creation (*kalpas*) characterized as a day in the life of Brahmā. At the end of each age, the universe is destroyed by fire and Brahmā enters into a time of slumber. During Brahmā's sleep, the universe is characterized as submerged in the cosmic waters until it is created anew.[15] A *kalpa* or day of Brahmā is equivalent to 4,320,000,000 years as we count them. This is also the measure of a night.[16]

A further example of a myth that foreshadows modern science is that of seeing creation as made up of an infinite number of universes residing within one another like nested boxes. On the scale of the small is found the electron, which contains within itself an entire universe. On the larger scale is our Universe. However, our Universe would be seen as but a single particle if we were able to enter the next higher universe. Carl Sagan ponders whether we may enter this higher universe by entering the fourth dimension.[17]

Correlations between, not myth, but Eastern mysticism and modern physics, are noted by another scientist, Fritjof Capra. He sees operative in both atomic physics and Eastern mysticism the principles of unity and dynamism.[18] Included under the principle of unity are the phenomena of interconnectedness, complementarity, and space-time.

According to Capra, interconnectedness is very apparent at the atomic level, where that which was regarded by classical physics (from Newton on) as solid objects "dissolve into patterns of probabilities, and these patterns do not represent probabilities of things, but rather probabilities of interconnections. Quantum theory forces us to see the universe not as a collection of physical objects, but rather as a complicated web of relations between the various parts of a unified whole."[19] Some Eastern mystics experience the world in this same way. In regard to complementarity, Capra proposes that in mysticism, opposites are seen as polar — as different aspects of the same phenomena. Thus, for example, yin and yang are perceived as aspects of Tao. This same idea is present in atomic physics, where matter and radiation exhibit both a particle and a wave aspect. Both aspects are needed if we are to have a full description of the one reality.[20] In regard to space-time, Capra finds that Eastern mysticism and modern physics show "that all the concepts we use to describe nature are limited, that they are not features of reality, as we tend to believe, but creations of the mind; parts of a map, not of a territory."[21] Eastern mysticism moves beyond our everyday understanding of space and time through meditation. Modern physics moves beyond our everyday understanding of space and time to an understanding of a realistic four-dimensional universe seen in terms of space-time.[22]

The second principle that Capra sees operative in both atomic physics and Eastern religions is the principle of dynamism. For example, the Cosmos is conceived by the Eastern mystics in dynamic terms involving movement, flow, and change. At the subatomic level, it is the nature of particles to be in motion; in fact, the more a particle is confined, the faster its velocity. On the cosmic level, it is the nature of the stars, the galaxies, and the Universe as a whole to be in motion and changing. Further, the Hindu myth of the expanding and contracting universe with each new creation involving unimaginable amounts of time is parallel to some "Big Bang" theories and their model of an expanding and contracting Universe. (In Hinduism this is referred to as *Lila,* the divine play.)[23] Another comparison is invited in that in Eastern mysticism, that which is called the Void is "the essence of all forms and the source of all life."[24] Field theories also indicate an underlying unity where matter is the transient manifestation of those places where the field is most intense.[25] A particularly striking manifestation occurs in vacuums, where virtual particles appear in the void and disappear back into it.[26] In Hinduism, the cosmic dance of creation is depicted as the dance of Shiva, who calls forth creation through sound and destroys it by fire while simultaneously holding all through the rhythm of the dance. In subatomic physics, the creation and destruction of particles produced in bubble chambers are a twentieth century visual form of the dance of Shiva.[27] For the Eastern mystic, change and transformation are seen as primary, and the structures and symmetries that these changes generate as secondary. This is also true in the world of subatomic physics where movement, transformation, and change are primary, and particles are "transient stages in an ongoing cosmic process."[28] Eastern mysticism sees all phenomena as interrelated and self-consistent.[29] Modern physics also sees all phenomena as interconnected and recognizes that "in order to explain any one of them we need to understand all the others."[30] Several schools of Eastern mysticism deny that there are any fundamental constituents of matter.[31] An analogous situation exists in modern physics, where the mechanistic worldview has been explicitly rejected and replaced by theories which see the universe "as a dynamic web of interrelated events."[32]

Capra concludes his presentation of the similarities of Eastern mysticism and subatomic physics by noting our need for a cultural revolution if we are to survive. He sees this survival resting "on our ability to adopt some of the yin attitudes of Eastern mysticism; to experience the wholeness of nature and the art of living with it in harmony."[33]

Before going on to our next section on modern science, it might be well to note David Maclagan's observation that creation myths are both ontogenetic and cosmogonic; that is, they are to be invoked when any new thing is brought into existence. They understand, explicitly or implicitly, that every *how* calls for a *why*. The myths that deal with the Cosmos may be imaginative stories or the constructs of science. A major difference between mythmakers and scientists is that scientists often do not see that they are coming out a myth—a human construct.[34] Neither mythmakers nor scientists tell the story as it might be told by the Creator, because they are embedded within the Cosmos, not apart from it.

Modern Science and Cosmology

Today within the discipline of science there is some movement to take a more holistic approach. This is evidenced both in the thinking about the various scientific disciples and their relation to one another, and in the thinking about science itself and its relationship to other disciplines such as theology. The former is exemplified in the work of Ilya Prigogine and Isabelle Stengers, who are working toward a unification of the two basic descriptions of nature: that of dynamics (classical physics), which applies to the world of motion, and that of thermodynamics, which he describes as "the science of complex systems with its intrinsic direction of evolution toward increasing entropy."[35]

Erich Jantsch, following the thought of Prigogine and Stengers, also argues for the emergence of a new scientific paradigm—one based on homologous principles (principles related through their common origin). This paradigm would link biological, socio-biological, and socio-cultural evolution. Jantsch suggests that "this should not come as a surprise since the whole universe evolved from the same origin."[36]

The latter—the establishment of a relationship between science and theology—may be seen, for example, in the work of Stephen Toulmin: *The Return to Cosmology*. In this book, Toulmin sets forth the preconditions needed for a unified world-view. He argues that cosmology—the study of the universe as a whole—should not ignore science but use it.[37] This shift in the place and purpose of science is clarified if one contrasts the thinking of Laplace at the beginning of the nineteenth century to that of Werner Heisenberg in our own time. Laplace believed that, if the scientist could know the position and velocity of all that makes up the Universe at its beginning, then it would be possible to give the entire subsequent history of the whole of the Cosmos. This thinking put the scientist in the position of being outside the Universe as a spectator. Of course, there is no outside.[38] In contrast, Heisenberg's "principle of indeterminacy" established that observation cannot be a "one-way street": "However delicate and minuscule our acts of observation on any subatomic particle may be, they will alter the particle's existing position or momentum, and so limit the precision with which its current condition can be known."[39] The most apparent example of science as a "two-way street" is the field of ecology, where one is always noticeably part of a system, as for example, in the food chain or in the prey-predator relationship.[40]

Prigogine and Stengers also argue for our embeddedness within the Cosmos but through consideration of the velocity in a vacuum of light (C) as a universal constant. They also consider it a limiting constant: "It limits the region in space that may influence the point where an observer is located."[41] "C" as a universal constant tells us that a signal cannot be transmitted at a velocity surpassing the speed of light. In other words, we are situated within—not without—the observed world; we are a part of nature.[42]

With the above as the context, we now turn to the main themes of this section, which is an examination of the origin of the Cosmos, the Earth's place in our present Universe, the issue of life on our Earth, and possible ends of the Cosmos.

Astronomers today operate out of an understanding of the beginning of the Universe so widely accepted that it is referred to as the standard model. The popular name for the standard model is the Big Bang. However, it is to be understood that this is not an explosion that started at a center and spread outward, but one that happened "simultaneously, everywhere, filling all space from the beginning, with every particle of matter rushing apart from every other particle."[43] This explosion involved an incomprehensible outpouring of energy composed mainly of the glow of photons, which together with electrons, positrons (positively charged electrons), and neutrinos were the most abundant particles in the early Universe. There were no molecules, atoms, or even the nuclei of atoms, because the temperature was too hot to enable them to bond.[44] This standard cosmological model of the Universe is based on two understandings derived from experiment. The first is an understanding that the Universe is expanding, an interpretation of the observed red shift.[45] In an expanding Universe, the galaxies are moving apart from one another at speeds proportional to their distances. But if the galaxies are all rushing apart, there must have been a time when they were closer together. Based on calculations using the Hubble constant (15 kilometers per second per million light years), it is determined that the Universe must be less than twenty billion years of age. This dating of the age of the Universe is supported by evidence from stellar evolution and from the rates of radioactivity which provide an age for our galaxy, the Milky Way, between ten and fifteen billion years.[46]

The second body of experimental data on which the standard cosmological model is based is the phenomenon of universal background radiation, technically referred to as black-body radiation.[47] If what had been predicted by theory from several sources—that the Universe had started with a "big bang"—were so, then there would exist background radiation of a certain temperature; this has been verified by experiment. The first verification occurred accidently in 1964 when two radio astronomers at Bell Telephone Laboratory in Holmdel, New Jersey, were attempting to measure the intensity of radio waves emitted from our own galaxy. The presence of this almost uniform background radiation has since been verified by a number of experiments by other scientists working with critical wavelengths.[48] According to Steven Weinberg, the fact that this radiation background noise is found at about 3 degrees Kelvin "allows us to determine the one crucial number that we will need to follow the history of the first three minutes."[49]

To look at the Universe at the age of 1/100th of a second and with a temperature of 100 billion degrees Kelvin would be to "see" a blaze of light of incomprehensible magnitude. It would be to see pure energy being converted to elementary particles—electrons, positrons, neutrinos, and photons—and these particles in turn being rapidly annihilated. It would be to see a small contamination of heavier particles: protons and neutrons.[50] It is not until the Universe is 700 thousand years old that it is cool enough for stable atoms to form and for radiation and matter to decouple and allow the formation of stars and galaxies. It will take about another ten billion years before the Earth creatures will begin to understand this story.[51]

Another way of looking at the beginning of the Universe is to see it as evolving out of a symmetry break. Erich Jantsch understands that at the beginning of this Universe there was symmetry, with the radiation and the matter/antimatter being transformed continuously into one another. Had this symmetry been perfectly maintained, we would have a Universe in which matter does not exist, but only radiation. The reality is that there was a symmetry break which resulted in an excess of matter particles estimated at a thousandth of a millionth (10^{-9}) of the original mass of matter. This resulted in the Universe as we know it today. Rather than a Universe whose energy is available almost totally in the form of radiation, our Universe is "matter-dominated" with its energy primarily invested in matter. This "clumping" occurred when the Universe had attained an age of approximately 700,000 years but was preceded by another break in symmetry—that between the physical forces.[52]

Theoretically, at least, at the "beginning" of the present Universe there was a basic symmetry among the four physical forces: the gravitational force which is now most operational at the macroscopic level, the electromagnetic force which is most observable in the intermediate range, and the nuclear forces (strong and weak) which act in the microscopic dimension.[53] With the break in symmetry between these four forces, the time-space continuum is unfurled. It is, in fact, the interplay of the physical forces which generates time-space.[54] The immediate consequence of the break in symmetry in the physical forces is the co-evolution of the Cosmos at the microscopic and macroscopic levels.[55]

> Macroscopic structures become the environment for microscopic structures and influence their evolution in decisive ways, or make it possible at all. Vice versa, the evolution of microscopic structures (nuclear, atomic and molecular syntheses) becomes a decisive factor in the formation and evolution of macroscopic structures. ... This principle [co-evolution] implies that every system is linked with its environment by circular processes which establish a feedback link between the evolution of both sides.[56]

It is in the stars that the principle of co-evolution of the microscopic and the macroscopic cosmos is apparent in an especially dramatic way.[57]

In addition to symmetry breaks between radiation/matter and the four physical forces, Jantsch contends that our Universe was able to emerge only because certain boundary conditions were met. These include the original high isotropy (uniformity in all directions), without which the forming structures would have been torn to pieces, and a limit velocity, without which the galaxies and their superstructures would have been prevented from forming. As in the macrocosmos, there are also very narrow boundaries in the microcosmos necessary for life to evolve. These include the relationship between the weak and the strong nuclear forces, which permitted the transformation of hydrogen into helium.[58] This is the process which fuels the stars, including our own star, the Sun.

The stars in a single galaxy are estimated to be on the order of a hundred billion. It is further estimated that there are a trillion galaxies altogether.[59] Our own home, the Milky Way, is a flattened disk 100,000 light years across. The Earth is located in one of the spiral arms of this galaxy in an area approximately thirty-three thousand light years from the central region.[60] The age of our Sun is 4,600 million years or about one-quarter of the age of the universe. It is probably a second or even third generation star.[61] It may be characterized as being in a stable state, a state that will last for about twelve billion years, at which time its supply of hydrogen will begin to diminish.[62] Ultimately, it will become a burned-out black dwarf star, but in the process it will give part of its mass to newly emerging stars and their planetary systems.[63] The Earth itself, and we humans, are probably made up, not of matter from our own star, but from the outer layers of the protosolar cloud and from stars which no longer exist.[64]

We are not unique. It has been estimated that approximately one-fourth of the stars in the Milky Way have a temperature comparable to that of the Sun, and it is possible that these twenty billion stars may have Earth-like planets. Outside the Milky Way galaxy and within the viewing power of the largest optical telescopes, there are 100 million galaxies. Given the fact that some of these galaxies are undergoing violent evolutionary processes that make life untenable, we are still left with billions of stars in the observable Universe that could provide an environment suitable for the development of a life-providing planet.[65] We have yet to encounter even one of them. At the present time, we Earthlings look in solitude to our own planet and to the Cosmos that she calls home for an understanding of the mystery we call life.

Freeman Dyson tells us: "The more I examine the universe and study the details of its architecture, the more evidence I find that the universe in some sense must have known that we were coming."[66] For example, the strength of the strong nuclear force lies within a range that makes life possible. If the strong nuclear force were slightly stronger, hydrogen would be a rare element and there would be no stars—like our Sun—which live by means of the slow burning of hydrogen. On the other hand, if the strong nuclear force were substantially weaker, it would not be possible for hydrogen to burn at all. A similar type of argument can be made in regard to the weak nuclear force. The weak nuclear force is just sufficient to allow the actual burning of hydrogen in the Sun to occur at a slow and steady rate, thereby making life possible. Also, the distances between the stars in our galaxy are such that we have not experienced the attraction of a nearby star; such an attraction would have made the four billion year old Earth journey that we are now experiencing the results of impossible. And finally, the exclusion principle, which states that two electrons cannot occupy the same state, makes the rich diversity of organic chemistry possible. Without this law, none of our essential chemistry could survive. Dyson says there are many other physical realities comparable to the preceding—realities which make life on Earth possible.[67]

Jantsch also presents his understanding of life in terms of a Universe that knew what it was about. He sees the beginning of life on Earth— microscopic evolution—as being made possible by the macrocosmos via the energy processes of the planetary environment, and perhaps by macrosystems beyond the planetary environment as evidenced by the organic traces found in meteorites and comets.[68] This co-evolution is also highly evident in the transformation of the biosphere and the atmosphere by the prokaryotes, nucleus-free single cells. Prokaryotes are responsible initially for the oxidation of the earth's surface and then for enriching the atmosphere with free oxygen. In turn, this transformation made possible the development of more complex life forms in the microcosmos. It also turned the biosphere and atmosphere into a self-regulating system (the Gaia hypothesis), which continues to maintain the conditions that make complex life on Earth possible—a maintenance in which these same prokaryotes still play their part.[69]

The Gaia hypothesis states that "the biosphere is a self-regulating entity with the capacity to keep our planet healthy by controlling the chemical and physical environment."[70] It sees the biosphere as being "more than just the complete range of all living things within their natural habitat of soil, sea, and air."[71] The Gaia hypothesis maintains that this complex system— living matter, soil, sea, and air—is in fact a single organism.[72] The atmosphere is an extension of the biosphere. The atmosphere is designed to maintain a certain environment comparable to the function performed by the nest for a wasp, feathers for a bird, and fur for a cat.[73] J. E. Lovelock argues that one of the most compelling arguments in support of the Gaia hypothesis is the continuous maintenance of a life-supporting climate for the past 3,500 million years—the time at which life began on the Earth. This favorable climate has been maintained despite a 25 percent or more increase in the Sun's energy.[74] Lovelock goes on to state:

> The biosphere's first exercise in actively modifying its environment may have been concerned with climate and the cooler sun, but there are other important environmental properties which have to be kept in subtle balance if life is to persist. Some essential elements are required in bulk, others in trace quantities, and all may need rapid redeployment at times; poisonous wastes and litter must be dealt with and, if possible, put to good use; acidity must be kept in check and a neutral to alkaline overall environment maintained; the seas should stay salt, but not too salt; and so on. These are the main criteria, but there are many others involved.[75]

We recognize the activity of Gaia when we find "on a global scale improbabilities in the distribution of molecules so unusual as to be different and distinguishable, beyond reasonable doubt, from both the steady state and the conceptual equilibrium state."[76] Examples of these global scale improbabilities in the distribution of molecules are found in the wood on our ground and in the oxygen and methane in the atmosphere.[77] A parallel way of looking for evidence of the activity of Gaia involves the use of a cybernetic mode.

> One of the most characteristic properties of all living organisms, from the smallest to the largest, is their capacity to develop, operate, and maintain systems which set a goal and then strive to achieve it through the cybernetic process of trial and error. The discovery of such a system, operating on a global scale and having as its goal the establishment and maintenance of optimum physical and chemical conditions for life, would surely provide us with convincing evidence of Gaia's existence.[78]

Lovelock finds evidence that the Gaian atmosphere operates as such a system, involving functions contributed by nitrogen, carbon dioxide, methane, nitrous oxide, ammonia, oxygen, and so on.[79] Also, the systems of the sea which, for example, maintain a constant salt content, may be another Gaian/cybernetic system.[80] Lovelock maintains that all cybernetic systems are intelligent in that "they must give the correct answer to at least one question."[81] So, as a cybernetic system, Gaia may also be characterized as intelligent.[82] Gaia is also creative in potentially disastrous situations, as, for example, that found in the impact of oxygen on anaerobic life two billion years ago. Gaia took this murderous intruder, oxygen, and converted it to a powerful friend that sustained life for aerobic creation.[83] The questions now before us are these: What part is the human called upon to play in the life-giving processes of Gaia? And, can we, have we already, made those processes impossible?

What seems to be needed is a new dialogue between the human and the natural world. For Prigogine and Stengers, this new dialogue is based on their finding in the natural world "essential elements of randomness and irreversibility. This leads to a new view of matter in which matter is no longer the passive substance described in the mechanistic world view but is associated with spontaneous activity."[84] They find that, in far-from-equilibrium states, matter seems to take into account the differences in the external world (differences such as electrical fields and weak gravitational fields) and to respond to them.[85] On the microscopic level, they cite the Heisenberg uncertainty principle as evidence for the breakdown of determinacy. But this breakdown is also occurring on the macroscopic level, for example, in living systems in which randomness can be found in non-equilibrium systems. They also cite the analogy which exists between the wave behavior of elementary particles and the wave behavior of chemical clocks.[86] This same type of self-organization behavior may be observed in slime molds when food becomes scarce. Any given amoeba may start the process with the other amoebas serving as relay providers.[87]

We have journeyed from the Universe's beginning as a fantastic out-pouring of energy through the formation of matter, the stars, the galaxies, and finally to life in our own galaxy, the Milky Way, and our own planet, Gaea. But there is yet one part of the story to be told. Given the present acceptance of the standard cosmological model, will it all end someday, and if so, how? The answer appears to depend on just how much matter there is in the Universe. If the cosmic density is less than the critical density, the Universe will go on expanding forever.[88] Within immense eons of time, as the galaxies moved farther and farther apart, we would become more and more alone in the night sky. On the other hand, if the critical density is above a certain level, at a certain point in time, it will begin to contract, possibly to continue an endless number of contracting and expanding cycles numbering billions of years each. Until we can accurately measure the amount of matter in the Universe, we will not know whether we live in an open or closed system. However, there is some evidence that we exist at a time when we have completed about one-tenth of a cycle, and that we will change from an expanding to a contracting Universe in another ten billion years.[89] Jantsch postulates that the evidence for a pulsating universe can be found in the presence of vast amounts of dark gaseous matter here—in amounts ten to twenty times heavier than the luminous matter in the universe. The theory of a pulsating Universe would also account for the large number of photons present in the Universe.[90] In this model of the pulsating universe, there is still the question of whether there will be—or ever was— a state of infinite density. Rather, at a time of finite density, the Universe may begin yet another expansive state after the period of contraction.[91] Bernard Lovell notes:

> Since the acceptance of the evidence that the Universe has evolved from a high-temperature initial condition, a great amount of work has been devoted to possible theoretical constructions whereby the singularity at time zero is avoided—for example, by transference to a previous cyclic phase of the Universe before the quantization of the gravitational field becomes important (say, at times less that 10^{-23} seconds).[92]

These journeys backward and forward over unimaginable distances and time put us in touch with mystery. But let us not forget that this mystery exists as truly in our own backyard as at "the first three minutes"—or the last. As Annie Dillard tells us:

> All this means that the physical world as we understand it now is more like the touch-and-go creek world I see than it is like the abiding world of which the mountains seem to speak. The physicists' particles whiz and shift like rotifers in and out of my microscope's field, and

that this valley's ring of granite mountains is an airy haze of those same particles I must believe. The whole universe is a swarm of those wild, wary energies, the sun that glistens from the wet hairs on a muskrat's back and the stars which the mountains obscure on the horizon but which catch from on high in Tinker Creek. It is all touch and go. The heron flaps away; the dragonfly departs at thirty miles an hour; the water strider vanishes under a screen of grass; the muskrat dives, and the ripples roll from the bank, and flatten, and cease altogether.[93]

The Universe as the Body of the Divinity

Some creation myths seem naturally to invite the hearers to experience Creation as sacred. For example, in Hindu mythology the Creation of the world is brought about by the self-sacrifice of the Divinity, with *sacrifice* used in its original meaning of "making sacred." Through this creative and recurring action, the Divinity becomes the World which, in time, again becomes the Divinity.[94] This view of all of Creation as sacred was also central to the religion of the Goddess.[95] And we in North America are learning from the Native Peoples about their understanding of Creation as sacred. However, it appears that this understanding of Creation as sacred will not be easily incorporated into Christianity. What seems to stand in our way is the most basic dualism of all — cosmic dualism.

Cosmic dualism is defined by Grace Jantzen as that dualism which postulates "a God of ultimate value and a material universe of no intrinsic worth."[96] Doctrinally, this cosmic dualism is expressed as *creatio ex nihilo*. All other dualisms can be deduced logically from this doctrine: male/female, technology/nature, mastery/slavery, clerical/lay, mind/body, thought/feeling.[97] Jantzen argues that the primary dualism — God/World —

was itself constructed as a theological justification for patriarchy. The dominant group of ruling class males constructed a world-view which set them apart as normative humanity, over against the "other" — women, other races, the poor, the earth — and then fashioned in their own image a God of ultimate value, power and rationality over against the disvalue, passivity and irrationality of the opposite side of the duality.[98]

According to Jantzen, the doctrine of *creatio ex nihilo* is not found in the Bible. Rather, it is at odds with the biblical accounts, which show the divine Spirit forming the Cosmos out of chaos.[99] The cosmic dualism between God and the World is philosophical in its roots, found initially in Plato and, more recently, Descartes. Theologically, it is grounded in teachers as diverse as Origen and Augustine, who held that man's creation in God's image pertained to his mind only and not to his body.[100] Rather, we can look upon *creatio ex nihilo* as "a theistic label to the mystery of why there should be something rather than nothing."[101] Jantzen argues that God forms the universe out of himself rather than out of nothing; the Cosmos is God's self-formation.[102]

Jantzen looks at the traditional doctrines of the Divine as omniscient (all-knowing), omnipotent (all-powerful), and omnipresent in light of her understanding of the World as God's body.[103] In regard to the first—omniscience—she speaks in terms of perception and embodiment. She cites the two traditional beliefs from Christian theology: that God is omniscient, and that God experiences all things directly. She argues that regarding God as embodied enhances rather than detracts from these traditional understandings. As humans, what we understand directly are the thoughts and feelings which occur within our own bodies. All else is mediated knowledge. What is within is direct, while the without is indirect. For God, all is within and direct.[104] Second, in regard to omnipotence, Jantzen speaks in terms of action and embodiment. She cites the two traditional beliefs from Christian theology: that God is omnipotent, and that the action of God is direct. Actions are direct because they occur within God's own body. Evil also resides within the body of God. Jantzen says her theologizing leaves the problems of natural laws and evil in the same place where traditional theism posits them; ontologically, God is ultimately responsible.[105] Third, when Jantzen speaks of omnipresence and embodiment, she sees omnipresence, not in terms of permeation, but rather as loving presence and ability to intervene at all times. The doctrine of omnipresence has to do with grace and immanence. As is true of humans also, some occurrences are more relevatory of the Divine Presence than are others.[106]

Rather than a model of cosmic dualism, Jantzen employs a model using the one and the many. She sees reality as one, not two, because nothing exists outside of the Divinity.[107] She also sees reality as many because the Divinity, who is creative love, "gives autonomy to that which it creates."[108]

Another way of looking at the Universe as the body of the Divine is not by way of overcoming cosmic dualism, but by bringing deeper understanding to the issue of immanence/transcendence. Jantzen suggests that the opposite of transcendence is not immanence but rather reductionism. Rather than seeing transcendence as other, she appears to see it as meaning that God is more than the sum of parts; that is, transcendence is seen in terms of "more than" rather than as "other." She uses the human as transcendent for the model of the transcendence of the Divinity.[109] We can use this insight of the whole being more than the sum of its parts whether we are speaking of a hydrogen atom, a mathematical construct, an elephant, or the Universe as the body of the Divinity. To reduce anything to merely its parts involves its destruction; like Humpty-Dumpty, "it" would no longer be.

As well as seeing immanence/transcendence in terms of the many, and the whole which is more than the sum of its parts, we can also deepen our understanding of the Cosmos as sacred by viewing immanence/transcendence in terms of known/unknown. As is pointed out by sources as diverse as Starhawk and the *Baltimore Catechism*, the Divinity inhabits every part of the Universe. Because of this embodiment of the Divinity, everything has inherent value. It is gift, not something that one can earn.[110] What this understanding of immanence seems to be saying is that we can know the Creator through knowing Creation. But there is also a sense in which the Divinity is transcendent—cannot be known. This may be expressed in terms of the ground of being as empty—empty because everything has been given over to the Universe. In other words, "all existence has been poured forth."[111] Since no-thing is left, there is no-thing to be known.

Finally, our understanding of the Universe as the body of the Divinity may be enhanced if we look at immanence/transcendence in terms of presence/absence. While Jürgen Moltmann does not speak of creation as the body of the Divinity, his theology could be developed in that direction through his understanding of the Creation as the presence of God.[112] He sees in the *Shekhina*, the feminine presence of the Divinity in the Kabbala, "the direct presence of God in the whole material world and in every individual thing within it."[113] Some would contend that our only knowledge of the Divine comes through her. And, in the eyes of both some Jewish and some Christian theologians, there is a close correlation between the action of the *Shekhina* and the Holy Spirit. In conjunction with the absence of the Divinity, the Kabbala speaks of the withdrawal of Yahweh into heaven while the *Shekhina* remains present and shares the suffering of Creation.[114] Today, this intense suffering is not only experienced by humanity, but by the very Earth itself.

In conclusion, it may be said that the above ways of looking at the Universe as the body of the Divine—by way of overcoming cosmic dualism and by way of an enhanced understanding of immanence/transcendence—may be classified as panentheistic; that is, they see the Cosmos as a part of the Divine, but they do not see the Divine as totally defined by the Cosmos. The challenge for Christian theologians is how this particular story relates to the universal story of the Cosmos as seen through the eyes of science.

The New Story/A New Story

For the first time in our recorded history, the whole Earth community has a single origin story.[115] This cosmic creation story provides the fundamental context that gives meaning to all the Earth's enterprises, including the human. We all can know and share the basic story about the stars, the planets, the galaxies, life forms, minerals, and human cultures. Within this universal context, we celebrate our unique spiritualities, histories, cultures, and so on.[116] A metaphor encompassing both the universal story and each particular story is brought to mind when one reflects on the curvature of the Earth: it is a curving that is tight enough to hold us all in its embrace but loose enough to foster creativity.[117] It is the Universe itself which is the "primary religious reality, the primary sacred community, the primary revelation of the divine, the primary subject of incarnation, the primary unit of redemption, the primary referent in any discussion of reality or of value."[118] The Universe is the context in which the divine reality found in the diverse religions is revealed to itself.[119] The Universe is both a psychic-spiritual as well as a material-physical reality.[120]

As some of us are tentatively beginning the dialogue of science and religion, it may be helpful to remember that this is not something new.[121] Rather, physics is rooted in the Greek philosophy of the sixth century B.C.E. when there was no separation among science, philosophy, and religion. The concern of physics was the discovery of the essential nature of things — a concern similar to that of mysticism. The sages of the Milesian school in Ionia were seen as "hylozoists" (those who think matter is alive). For them, there was no distinction between spirit and matter, the animate and inanimate; rather, all was pulsing with life. Thus, Thales declared that all objects were full of the divinity, and Anaximander saw the universe as a living organism permeated by *pneuma*, the cosmic breath or spirit.[122]

In our own time, many are putting their hand to the writing of the New Story. Here we will listen to the voices of three people, the first, that of Thomas Berry, the first to teach many of us the New Story.

> The story of the universe is the story of the emergence of a galactic system in which each new level of expression emerges through the urgency of self-transcendence. Hydrogen in the presence of some millions of degrees of heat emerges into helium. After the stars take shape as oceans of fire in the heavens, they go through a sequence of transformations. Some eventually explode into the stardust out of which the solar system and the earth take shape. Earth gives unique expression of itself in its rock and crystalline structures and in the variety and splendor of living forms, until humans appear as the moment in which the unfolding universe becomes conscious of itself. The human emerges not only as an earthling, but also as a worldling. We bear the universe in our beings as the universe bears us in its being. The two have a total presence to each other and to that deeper mystery out of which both the universe and ourselves have emerged.[123]

Or, in words of Mary Southard, an artist:

> There is a revelation occurring today which is one of the greatest in the history of the human species. This event is happening in a most unlikely place: in science! Scientists are uncovering the wonderful dynamics and structure of "matter," the precision of the unfolding of

creation, the care and balance of each step of evolution, the presence of creative energy within all creatures from the smallest to the greatest, the music in the rocks, the dance of the stars, the explosion and extravagance of life, the miracle of Earth.

This revelation—this New Story—speaks of the universe as created from WITHIN where all is therefore sacred from the beginning![124]

And finally, physicist Brian Swimme describes the movement from mechanistic science to an understanding of science as mystery as:

the encounter with the ultimacy of no-thing-ness that is simultaneously a realm of generative potentiality; the dawning recognition that the universe and Earth can be considered as living entities; the awareness that the human person, rather than a separate unit within the world, is the culminating presence of a billion-year process; and the realization that, rather than having a universe filled with things, we are enveloped by a universe that is a single energetic event, a whole, a unified, multiform, and glorious outpouring of being.[125]

In all three stories of the Universe, mention is made of the human. It is to the role of the human in the story of the Universe that we now direct our attention.

If the human were to be defined within the context of the Universe, it could be said that "we are the universe in its self-awareness phase."[126] We need both the physical-material and the psychic-spiritual as the two dimensions from which human consciousness emerges; this is a consciousness which is both reflective and celebratory.[127] Put in another way, it may be said that it is the job of the human "to create the human form of the central powers of the cosmos."[128] These central powers are defined by Brian Swimme as allurement, sea, land, life forms, fire, and wind.[129] The cosmic power of allurement is the most primordial of these powers. All is grounded in attraction, whether it is the force of gravity or human love. Without this attraction, the Cosmos would literally come apart.[130] The second power, the power of the sea, may be seen as its power to dissolve the Universe. Swimme calls this power the power of sensitivity—the power to take in the "other" and really be changed by it. He also uses the example of the electron and the proton and "quantum stickiness" wherein the proton absorbs something from the electron and in the process becomes something new.[131] The third power, the power of the land, may be seen in its power to remember. "For the cosmos, memory is the way the past *works* in the present."[132] In remembering, as the Cosmos does, we put ourselves in touch with infinite beauty and power. Matter does this remembering through DNA.[133] Life, the fourth power mentioned, teaches us that adventurous play is the true habitat of the human. We are the life form that never really grows up, a dynamic referred to as neatony. The Cosmos itself plays; it creates in a random way that is not predictable.[134] The fifth power, that of fire, is seen as the Cosmic dynamic of unseen shaping. It is why something may be called a self, whether it is a human, an atom, a tornado, or the Earth itself. We see this dynamic at work in the Earth's ability to maintain a steady temperature—one favorable to life—for over three billion years, despite the fact that the sun's temperature has risen at least 25 percent. It is also evidenced by the prokaryotes' creation of the correct percentage of oxygen for animal life.[135] The sixth and final force, that of wind, is seen as the cosmic dynamic of celebration as announcing. At the beginning, the Universe was concentrated in a "pin-point," which burst out and has been expanding ever since.[136] "We are Generosity-of-Being evolved into human form."[137]

The preceding part of this section has looked primarily at the universal story and has touched on the interrelationship between this story and the stories which are particular to each group. I will close by addressing briefly the input from one particular group—that of Christians.

Specifically, Christian theology can make a contribution to cosmology by asking the right questions and pointing to some possible answers. Scientist Stephen Hawking has already given theology one question when he asks: If space and time form a closed surface without boundary—if they are neither created nor destroyed—what is the role of the Divine?[138] One possible direction to pursue in answering this question is suggested by the Kabbala.[139] It would involve the idea of the withdrawal of the Holy One (the transcendent one who is creative force) and the leaving behind of the immanent one (the Word and the Spirit). This withdrawal could be correlated to the "Big Bang." Of course, this would not be a satisfactory reply to Hawking and the others who have moved away from the idea of a "Big Bang" singularity.

A second, and probably even more significant question for Christian theology is this: What is the role of the Divinity today? It appears that the Divinity continues to create. Specifically, we may see Creation continuing to take place through the Word, who differentiates, and the Spirit, who unites. This points to the role of the human, also—to be responsible co-creators in the evolving mystery of Life. In this we receive encouragement from the work of Ilya Prigogine, for example, who has shown that, in systems far from equilibrium, a small input may result in a significant change.[140] We certainly live in a system far from equilibrium and—if Prigogine and Strengers are right—what will happen would appear to be up to us acting with the Spirit and the Word.

I close with the beginning of a beginning story:

Before the beginning, the Holy One gave herself over entirely to her Spirit and to her Word. The cosmos is the result of this emptying out of herself. Because of this emptying out, she cannot be known. But we can know her Word and her Spirit. There exists no particle, no tree, no bird, no life-form, no galaxy, no void which they do not fill. In knowing them, it may be said that we know Her. She is the Holy One about whom we can say no-thing. We stand in silence and in awe.

PART 3

THE DIVINE

5.

The Holy Spirit as the Feminine Divine

My Ph.D. studies began with a course by Bernard Häring on the experience of the Holy Spirit in our lives and culminated with the writing of a dissertation entitled "The Holy Spirit in Whiteheadian Process Theologians." In the between times, I was not overly conscious of Her presence, but hindsight makes me more aware of it. However, Her presence became more and more real for me as I wrote the dissertation. I first articulated this to myself when I had to make the choice of a pronoun to describe the Holy Spirit: Was the Spirit He, She, or It? A deep looking within to my experience of the Holy Spirit revealed that, for me, the Spirit is a feminine presence. Ultimately, mainly for political reasons and because I knew of nowhere in the Christian scriptures and tradition where the Holy Spirit was addressed as She, I chose to call Her "It." However, I did so with the promise that, after graduation, I would go back and investigate the scripture and tradition to see if anything recorded there resonated with my own religious experience of the Holy Spirit as feminine. I found enough to form the basis for a book, *Created in Her Image: Models of the Feminine Divine*, which I co-authored with Bernice Marie-Daly.

In that book, for me, a key insight came from Yves Congar's statement in reference to Genesis 1:27 and the creation of male and female in the image of the Divine. Congar stated: "If this is true, then there must be in God, in a transcendent form, something that corresponds to masculinity and something that corresponds to femininity."[1] For me, this femininity was expressed through the Holy Spirit, and women were particularly those who were *Created in Her Image*. However, since the writing of that book, my vision has become less human centered; I now try to view things not only from the point of view of the human, but also from the point of view of the Cosmos. In this chapter, I try to incorporate that larger vision, as well as articulate new insights gained from a theological perspective.

Why the Divine as Feminine?

Elsewhere I have argued for the parallels that exist between the imaging and treatment of women and the Earth, and how our images of the Divine are related to the experiences of women and the Earth.[2] My own conviction of the interconnectedness of these three issues has grown to the point where I have established the Center for Women, the Earth, the Divine, which is devoted to the exploration of this interconnectedness. At this point in time, I think that there is a growing realization that we are going to have to work *both* on changing the status of women and the Earth *and* on changing our language and symbols of the Divine. In other words, changing the status of the Earth and women will not necessarily lead to changes in the Divine language and symbol systems, nor will changing the Divine language and symbol system necessarily lead to positive changes for women and the Earth.[3] Rather, it seems to me that the call to all women today is to put themselves into that part of the process for change where they can be most effective—while never losing sight of the whole new world-view that we are all struggling for.

For me, the key to the changes for which we struggle resides in our ability to posit a true feminine as not just valuable but as ultimately valuable.[4] This comes out of my understanding that all of us, theists and atheists alike, live out of a world-view based on that which we consider to be of ultimate value. And that we all, as the Psalmist said of the pagans in Psalm 115:8, become like the gods that we worship. Or, as Donald Gelpi has stated so well and succinctly: "For we become what we worship, since we worship what we value ultimately and absolutely."[5] If this is the case, it leads me, as a Christian theist, to at least two conclusions. First, it means that who the Divinity is becomes the ultimate practical issue. And it leads me to the necessity for positing the feminine, as infinite value, within the Divinity itself. Precisely what this feminine will encompass will have to come from the lived experiences of all women, with the understanding that being a woman is, for us, a primary source of revelation. We won't understand who the Holy Spirit is until we, as a minimum, get her gender right![6] But She is more than the feminine, as valuable as this is in supplying metaphors for Her such as Sister, Daughter, Mother, the New Eve, Friend. In other words, while She may be said to embody explicitly the feminine presence in the Divine and in the Cosmos, She implicitly embodies the masculine presence also.[7] Further, metaphors without gender, such as Fire, Water, Wind, Power, also give us insight into who She is.

While acknowledging that the feminine does not tell us everything that there is to say about the Holy Spirit, it does tell us something critical concerning Her. The rest of this chapter looks at what it means in regard to Her function (mission), Her relationship to Christ, Her relationships within the Trinity, and Her person. It is to Her mission or function that we now turn.

The Function of the Holy Spirit

Historically, because of the teachings of the *Pneumatomachoi*, the first theological speculation on the Holy Spirit was directed toward Her person and not Her mission. In fact, the question of the function of the Holy Spirit still remains a matter in need of adequate theological formulation.[8] What the rendering of an official statement concerning Her divinity did accomplish was the acknowledgment that the Holy Spirit is supremely worthy of our adoration. But this declaration occurred at the price of shutting off further speculation on Her person—what kind of a proper name is *Holy Spirit?*—and on Her function, an issue that is beginning to be addressed today as evidenced, for example, by the choice of the Holy Spirit for the theme of the Seventh General Assembly of the World Council of Churches.[9]

Elsewhere I have written on the function of the Holy Spirit in the church and the world.[10] What I wish to do in this section is not to repeat what I have already said, but rather to emphasize three functions of the Holy Spirit that I see as particularly in need of further development. These are Her cosmic function, Her function in regard to Mary of Nazareth, and Her function in regard to universal salvation.

From a Christian perspective, the first encounter with the Spirit in the Hebrew scriptures finds Her moving over waters of chaos (Genesis 1:2). Her function as a cosmic creative life-force reappears periodically in the scripture, for example in Psalm 33:6 and Psalm 104:27-30, and reaches its climax in the Wisdom literature.[11] In Wisdom 7:21-8:1, the scriptural theologies of the Spirit and Wisdom "meet and are identified."[12] Here Wisdom is spoken of in terms that are usually reserved for the Divinity alone. She is everywhere, orders all things well, and can do all things. This cosmic function is also made explicit in Sirach 24:3b-6. In this passage, Kathleen O'Connor sees the Wisdom Woman in a function of universality in which She claims a unique relationship to the Earth itself and is "in the center of a matrix of relationships."[13] O'Connor further sees Sirach 24 as making the identification between the Wisdom Woman and the Divinity explicit.[14]

The second mentioned function of the Holy Spirit, which is in regard to Mary of Nazareth, has been presented at length by Leonardo Boff in *The Maternal Face of God*[15] and briefly in *Trinity and Society*. Using the Lukan text "The Holy Spirit will come upon you" (Luke 1:35) as a starting place for his theological hypothesis, he sees the Holy Spirit as taking on a human form in Mary in the same manner as the Word took on human form in Jesus. Through this action of the Spirit, Mary was divinized and truly is the Mother of God. Just as the Son divinized maleness explicitly and femaleness implicitly, the Holy Spirit [Daughter?] divinized femaleness explicitly and maleness implicitly. The Holy Spirit is personally present to Mary just as the Son is incarnate in Jesus.[16] It is the destiny of women (and men through their feminine side) to be divinized by the Holy Spirit as Mary was, "to the extent proper to each person."[17] In secular terms, this divinization seems to be what Jantsch is referring to when he speaks of true creativity as residing in our ability to overcome the dualism between the creator and the created.[18]

As Boff used Luke 1:35 for the starting point for his theological hypothesis on the function of the Holy Spirit in regard to Mary, so one might start with Luke 7:35 and develop a theological hypothesis on the function of the Holy Spirit in regard to Her role as universal giver of salvation. Luke 7:35 presents Jesus as saying: "Yet Wisdom is justified by all her children." In the verses preceding this (7:18-34), Jesus contrasts the lifestyles of himself and John, John's being that of an ascetic and Jesus' being that of one who came "eating and drinking" (7:34). What each of them did was bring a message of salvation that was heard by some, while others rejected the messages of both John and Jesus. In sighting Wisdom as being justified by *all* of her children, could Jesus be suggesting that it is Wisdom who is the universal saving presence?[19] Thus She would be seen as justified by John and Jesus and the rest of her children.[20]

The Spirit/Word Relationship

There are three perspectives from which one may look at the Spirit/ Word relationship. One may look at it from the point of view of the Spirit, wherein the function of the Word is to reveal to us who the Spirit is. This is the understanding of Donald Gelpi, who sees Jesus revealing to us the Holy Spirit as "the divine mind who is the Holy Breath."[21] Or, as has most frequently been done, beginning with John 15:26 one may look at the Spirit/ Word relationship from the focus of the Word, where the function of the Spirit is to reveal to us who the Word is.[22] Or, one may look at the relationship as one which is mutually revelatory, which would seem to be called for because the radical reality of both Spirit and Word is to be the Divinity. It is on this third model—where the distinctness of the Word and the Spirit is honored, as well as their unity—that this section will focus.

Following Congar in regard to Genesis 1:26-27, it may be stated that if creation is in the image of the Holy One, and if the Holy One creates female/male, then there must be in the Divinity itself something which corresponds to femininity and something which corresponds to masculinity.[23] I suggest that the femininity is to be found explicitly in the Holy Spirit and the masculinity explicitly in the Word. Following this lead, let us look at some of the ways in which a relationship of mutuality is played out by Spirit and Word in the scriptures. For example, commenting on Genesis 1:2, Moltmann states: "The Word specifies and differentiates, the Spirit Unites and creates harmony. As with human speech, the words—utterances—are different but are imparted in the same breath."[24]

In Psalm 33:6-7, a reversal occurs in that the work of the Word comes before that of the Spirit. In addition, it is the Spirit who has taken on the function of differentiation—of bringing form.[25] Turning from the psalms to the history of Israel, we find in George Montague the telling insight that before the Kings ruled in Israel, the emphasis was on the Spirit. But when the Kings ruled, the emphasis was on the Word. This seems to be the result of a growing concern for orthodoxy.[26] It might also be seen in terms of a concern for order *vs.* a concern for creativity. The above indicates that both the Word and Spirit are concerned with order and creativity—the Word with order explicitly and creativity implicitly and the Spirit with creativity explicitly and order implicitly?

The strongest contrast between the spirit as nonrational (the dream) and the word as rational (the spoken media) is found in Jeremiah 23:25-29. In his concern about false prophesying, Jeremiah has gone to an extreme of overemphasis on the word, while avoiding any mention of the spirit as regards his own prophesying.[27] This stereotype of the feminine as nonrational and the male as rational is obviously still with us, with harmful consequences for both the human and the Earth. However, Jeremiah's rejection of the spirit is reversed in Joel 2:28-29; Joel tells us that all of humankind will receive the spirit. Joel also goes back to honoring dreams and visions. The spirit has here regained ascendancy over the word,[28] probably because Joel's times, like ours, were in need of this ascendancy. In Second Isaiah 40:6-8, a reversal of stereotype is seen in that the spirit is the spirit of judgment, of death, of destruction, while the word is the word of re-creation. Viewed as a whole, it may be seen that their joint actions are needed if the new creation is to become a reality.[29] This necessity for the presence of both spirit and word is seen explicitly in Third Isaiah 55:21, where we are told that to be in relationship with the Holy One involves both spirit and word. In summary, the Hebrew scriptures offer many examples of a mutual revelation of Spirit and Word—some that speak to stereotypes, some that break these modes by reversal, some that offer models of true complementarity. We now turn to the Christian scriptures in order to gain more insight into the Spirit/Word relationship.

It is primarily in the writings of Paul and John that we find actual teachings *on* the Spirit in contrast to Luke, for example, where an experience *of* the Holy Spirit is given.[30] For purposes of this section, it should be noted that Paul was able to present the life of Christ "without even mentioning the Spirit."[31] However, in Thessalonians 1:5, he does see the gospel as coming to us "not only in word, but also in power and in the Holy Spirit." And Paul does present the action of the Spirit and of Christ in the same terms—justification, righteousness, joy, love, peace, sanctification, speaking, fullness of life, indwelling, one body.[32] This same kind of paralleling between the action of the Spirit (Paraclete) and of Jesus is to be found in John's gospel. Thus both are seen as: given by the Father, with and in the disciples, experiencing a world that cannot receive them, known only to believers, sent by the Father, teaching, bearing witness, confounding the world, not speaking for themselves but speaking only what they have heard, glorifying, unveiling, and guiding into all truth.[33] Given these parallels between the actions of Spirit and Word, we are led to ask: Why two? Why the Holy Spirit and not just the glorified Jesus? What we seem to see here is an example of what Congar refers to as elsewhere as the "consistent pattern

in God's actions: namely, the proceeding by means of pairs or doublets."
There is in this pattern "something very profound, a kind of rule of the
divine Poeticus."[34]

A final example from the Christian scriptures, coming out of theological
speculation on the Lukan gospel (1:35), is Boff's argument for the divinization of Mary through her relationship to the Holy Spirit as the feminine
parallel to the divinization of Jesus through his relationship to the Word.[35]
This issue will be treated at greater length when, in the final section of this
chapter, we look at the person of the Holy Spirit.

Before leaving this section on the parallels that exist in the Spirit/Word
relationship, mention must be made of the *filioque* clause, which may be
perceived as standing in the way of the development of a full-blown Pneumatology. As long as the Western church, through the *filioque*, subordinates
the Spirit to the Word, it will not be possible to see Her as She truly is.
However, with the growing recognition by both the Protestant and the
Roman Catholic branches of Christianity of the historical and political reasons why this clause came into existence and their growing withdrawal of
its use, the *filioque* clause may eventually be removed as a deterrent for a
much-needed Pneumatology.[36] But it is not only in the West that a dominator model of Trinitarian theology is foremost, as exemplified by the *filioque* clause and its positing of power in the Son. A dominator model is
also prevalent in Eastern Christianity, with its monarchial model of the
Trinity and its positing of power in the Father. The movement from these
dominator models to the beginnings of a Trinitarian model that truly honors
the Holy Spirit as One worthy of our love and worship is the subject of the
next section.

The Holy Spirit and the Trinity

It is interesting that one can read articles and books on the Trinity and
never even find mention of the Holy Spirit—only of the Father and the
Son! It seems that we are entering the twenty-first century with only half
of a Trinitarian theology. I am reminded of a visiting priest who used to
come to my parish; a stroke had left one side of his body basically non-
functional. Without a theology that enables the life-giving Spirit to be available to us in Her fullness, we are like that priest and more so, because
more than our bodies are affected. The first step that must be taken if we
are to come into wholeness is to address the Holy Spirit as She. In addition,
we must look at the implications that this involves in regard to the triunity
of the Trinity, the "Father," the Word, the person of the Spirit, the meaning
for us. We now look at the insights shed on these issues, primarily by
Donald Gelpi, but with additional insights from other theologians, including
myself.

In *The Divine Mother*, Gelpi proposes the method of analogy with human social experience as the best basis for reaching an understanding of the triunity of the Holy One via theology.[37] His concern is to conceive of a way of preserving the vital identity of the Divine persons while preserving the personal autonomy that makes them distinct Divine selves. He sees the similarity of both the Divine and human persons residing in their existence in one another in life-giving ways; in their care for one another; in their exchange of mutual enthusiasms and insights. However, the human and the Divine differ in that we can be death-giving as well as life-giving and that we experience bodily separation. Nevertheless, there is something about this experience of giving of life to one another that leads one to say that it is not only the key to human life but to Divine life as well.[38] For the Divinity only, the use of the term *perichoresis* stands for the perfect mutual inexistence that constitutes their vital identity.[39] For humans, separated by their bodies, their histories, and their dissents, *perichoresis* stands for their vital similarity.[40]

In regard to the issue of seeing the Divinity as *Father*, there seems to be no difficulty in the use of this term on Gelpi's part. This is probably because he is able to retain this term and achieve gender balance through seeing the Holy Spirit as feminine and Jesus as androgynous. But before looking at his thinking on Jesus as androgynous, it is helpful to see what he has to say about the Word.

According to Gelpi, there are at least two meanings that can be given to the term *Logos* (Word). It can mean the mind of the Divine, and it can also stand for the spoken, or revealed, expression of the Divine. The issue then becomes which is the more appropriate understanding. Our agreement or lack thereof with Gelpi's understanding of the term *Logos* will be the basis for our acceptance or rejection of what he says about the Holy Spirit. Based on the scriptural evidence, Gelpi argues that it is the Divine Breath which is experienced as enlightenment or the Divine mind.[41] This path was followed by Irenaeus (c. 130-c. 200), who saw the Divine Wisdom as the one who nourishes, increases, and illumines, and the Son as the one who executes the will of the Father, while the Father is unknown, transcendent, and mysterious. This understanding of the Holy Spirit as enlightenment is developed by Gaius Marius Victorinus (baptized c. 354), who saw the Son as the action of the Father and the Spirit as His mind—the living thought of the Divine. Through the Son, the Divine being is channeled outward and downward into matter, while the Spirit is the Divine intelligence who leads us back to the Divinity.[42] Victorinus also "taught that when the New Testament tells us that Jesus was conceived by the Holy Breath, it asserts that She is mother of the Son in heaven and on earth."[43] For Gelpi, the Spirit's conception of the Word is an act of enlightenment, an act that is in the eternal now.[44] Gelpi further sees Victorinus as suggesting that the Second Person of the Trinity may be seen as androgynous—not only the Christ, but the Son in heaven. His commentary on Victorinus includes the following: while Jesus was certainly male, he showed himself to be Son of God not through his maleness, but through his obedience—a way open to all men and women; Jesus can reveal the Divine Mother to us only because, as a result of Her enlightenment, he becomes that which is feminine and therefore capable of revealing the feminine; the archetype of the androgyne stands for the reconciliation of opposites—female and male—that takes place in Christ, that is, the Divine Mother and the Divine Father may be legitimately imaged as acting through their androgynous Son to effect the "coincidentia oppositorum"; if the Word is androgynous, women represent the Word as much as do men, notably via sacramental action.[45]

Gelpi argues that we experience the Holy Spirit as enlightenment because it is through Her that we experience both the Lordship of Jesus and the Fatherhood of God.[46] Because Her historical mission was one of gracious enlightenment, She should be understood as being the mind of the Divinity. The biblical writers' tendency to describe the Holy Breath as the divine principle of saving enlightenment culminates in the Hebrew scriptures when She is perceived as transcendent Divine Wisdom and in the Christian scriptures in Paul where She is seen as the mind of God and of Christ (1 Corinthians 2:4-16).[47] Gelpi sees contemporary Pneumatology as largely untouched by the great number of scriptural references that he cites on the Holy Spirit as the intelligence of the Divinity. Rather, he sees it as reflecting Trinitarian theology as popularized in the Middle Ages, a theology that had, for historical reasons, largely forgotten many biblical truths about the Holy Spirit. What we inherited was an understanding of the Holy Spirit basically derived from a fusion of Christian faith and Platonic metaphysics.[48] It is due to the influence of neo-Platonism that "first rational, then gracious enlightenment was with increasing frequency appropriated to the *Logos*, to the Son, rather than to the Spirit."[49] As a result, who She was became very murky, obscure, mysterious, whereas the picture that we derive of Her from scripture as enlightenment is often very concrete.

As well as seeing the Spirit as Divine mind, Gelpi also presents Her as the Divine Mother. He bases his imaging of Her as Divine Mother in both theology and psychology. The theology comes out of an understanding that through the conception of Jesus by the Holy Breath, we are taught that She is the Mother of the Son in Heaven and on Earth; the psychology relies on the transvaluation of the archetype of the feminine. He sees this transvaluation as needed if we are to have a personal image of the Spirit, an image that is necessitated by Christian hope.[50]

Our proper response to the actions of the Holy Spirit is one of receptivity—receptivity to the "rushing wind that sweeps along the one whom it enlightens."[51] Further, in our awareness of mission—of being sent—we experience Her as the One who is sent.[52] In mission, we truly share in who She is.

In summary, it may be said that some of the positive aspects that Gelpi contributes toward a Trinitarian theology of a community of equals are his balance in seeing the Father as masculine, the Holy Spirit as feminine, and Jesus as androgynous; his emphasis on *perichoresis* as the meaning of unity rather than an emphasis on monarchy; his presentation of the biblical passages and historical development that free the Spirit to be enlightenment (Wisdom?) and the Word to be the One who does the will of the Divinity; his understanding of the Spirit as being involved in the conception of the Word; his insight that, if we are to relate to Her, we must be able to image Her as person. What is lacking is true balance, both in the life of the immanent Trinity itself because of the nature of the processions; and in the earthly expressions of the Trinity, where only a male expression is found: in the incarnation of the Word in Jesus. We will look at Boff to see what light he casts on these two issues and conclude by presenting a possible way of looking at the processions that reflects balance and not domination.

In regard to the latter issue — the lack of an earthly expression of the Divinity as explicitly feminine — Boff, as previously mentioned, offers his *theologoumena* (theological hypothesis) on the Holy Spirit as having taken on the specific form of Mary. We will address this hypothesis in the next section when we look at the person of the Holy Spirit. In regard to the former issue, Boff offers the following. Rather than seeing the Father as only Father, he contends that, in faithfulness to biblical language, we should present the One Source as the maternal Father/the paternal Mother.[53] For Boff:

> The Father reveals himself through the Son and the Holy Spirit as inviting, utterly mysterious depth, a mystery both paternal and maternal. The Father reveals the Son as his Word with the participation of the Spirit, who is always the Spirit of the Son and the Father. The Son is "begotten" by the Father in the Holy Spirit. Put figuratively, the Father "begets" the Son virginally in the maternal-virginal womb of the Holy Spirit. In trinitarian terms: the Father "begets" the Son *Spiritique*, that is, in communion with the Holy Spirit.[54]

While the above deals with gender balance, it suffers from the exclusive use of the terms *Father* and *Son* while not using the terms *Mother* and *Daughter*.[55] A possible way of looking at the processions that address this lack follows.

The Cappodocian-Byzantine *theologoumena*, regarding the procession of the Holy Spirit, is stated by Jean-Miguel Garrigues as follows: "The Spirit goes forth from the Father alone through the Son.[56] One could balance the processions by stating that the Son goes forth from the Mother alone through the Spirit. However, I think it would be better to speak of the Spirit going forth from the Mother (Father) alone through the Son and of the Son going forth from the Father (Mother) alone through the Spirit.[57] This is because the Spirit is explicitly a manifestation of the feminine energy of the Divinity, while the Son is explicitly a manifestation of the masculine energy of the Divinity. Implicitly, of course, they both manifest the other energy. It also should be noted, as does Garrigues, that origin is regarded as "the starting point of a continuous process" rather than the "principle from which a distinction issues."[58] Even our mathematics could help us here if, rather than using the symbol of an equilateral triangle to represent the Holy Trinity, we used a circle which stands for a process that is without beginning or ending but everywhere simultaneous. This idea of simultaneity is stated well by Boris Bobrinskoy:

> The "revelatory function" of the Holy Spirit allows us to say, as a counterbalance to the western diagram, that, if it is true that the Son is not extraneous to the procession of the Holy Spirit (without bringing in the idea of casuality), on the other hand neither is the Holy Spirit extraneous, exterior to the generation of the Son. One cannot separately conceive of or articulate the two eternal movements of the Trinity; one must remember, following the whole of Orthodox tradition both ancient and modern, that their character is concomitant (St. Gregory of Nyssa) and simultaneous (St. John Damascene). Any introduction, even purely conceptual and speculative, of anteriority in the generation of the Son relative to the procession of the Spirit, contributes to the rationalization and unbalancing of the trinitarian mystery, to the great hurt of the Church, in which the reign of the Trinity is inaugurated.[59]

We conclude this chapter by looking at the images that seem most appropriate when addressing the Holy Spirit as person.

The Person of the Holy Spirit

There are many images that we may use in speaking of the Holy Spirit. Two that speak to themes in this book are: "the principle that creates differences and communion"[60] (the one and the many), and the Holy Spirit as complete, unmediated Presence.[61] While these images, and many others that could be mentioned, are worthy of further development, in this section I concentrate on images of the Holy Spirit that emphasize Her as person. They include Mary as embodiment of the Holy Spirit; the Spirit as Wisdom Woman; the Holy Spirit as the feminine. But before looking at these images, we need to look at that much discussed, but little understood, issue of person. Obviously, it is beyond the scope of this book to make a definitive statement on the issue of person; however, it is necessary to shed enough light on the issue so that a context for theologizing on the Holy Spirit as person is established.

The history of the development of doctrine in Pneumatology shows us that it was only in time that the Holy Spirit came to be regarded as Divine.

Further, She is seldom regarded on Her own but rather almost always in a Trinitarian or a Christological context. Stereotypically, one is reminded of the image of marriage, where the two are one and that one is the husband! Thus, for example, the Council of Nicea said little about Her except to declare: "And we believe in the Holy Spirit." Among the Greek theologians, while Anthanasius did emphasize Her Divinity, he did not come to terms with who She is. Likewise, the Cappodocians (Basil, Gregory of Nazianzus, Gregory of Nyssa) defended Her Divinity but did little to advance an understanding of Her. Among the Latin theologians, Augustine proposed that we view the divine persons as relational realities with the Holy Spirit seen as the bond of love between the Father and the Son. (But is a bond of love a person?) The writings of Boethius were very influential in regard to person, but dealt basically with the person as intelligent rather than as also emotional or bodily. It is in Richard of St. Victor (twelfth century) that we find the beginning of the "modern" understanding of person as not only relational and intelligent, but also social and ecstatic. In other words, while we live in and through communion with one another, we are also unique in that each enjoys a particularity that cannot be communicated. Aquinas defended the relational character of persons as "subsistent relations," turning the noun, *substance*, into an adjective and the adjective, *relational*, into a noun.[62] This speaks to those of us today who view relationship as a primary reality. Thus, for example, for ecofeminists, to be means to be in relationship to or to be mutually inexistent (*perichoresis*). For purposes of contextualizing a theology on the person of the Holy Spirit, a descriptive analysis of the word *person* involves: self-awareness, real continuity, relational reality, conscious responsibility, and autonomy.[63]

For women explicitly our femininity, our femaleness is a primary source of revelation. And so, one is justified in suggesting, was it for Mary. In fact, since as a woman of her time Mary would not have been given the opportunity to study the scriptures in depth, we may surmise that her understanding of *Ruah* would have been almost wholly experiential. This experience was so deep that Mary could be totally open to the Holy Spirit to the point of enabling, for example, the conception of Jesus to take place. It may also be argued that she was open to the Holy Spirit to the point where the Spirit was enabled to take on the specific form of Mary.[64] Light may be shed on the Holy Spirit/Mary relationship by looking at the official teachings about her as set forth by Roman Catholic Christianity. The doctrine of the Immaculate Conception tells us that Mary was never under the influence of sin; that is, she was totally open to the Divinity and, also, was totally open to her full humanity. By declaring her full of grace, we are saying that the Divinity was given fully to Mary and that Mary has accepted this Divine life completely. The doctrine of Mary's perpetual virginity, taken in the context of her Jewish religion and culture which considered virginity a curse, may be seen as a sign of her emptiness. It speaks of her willingness to be the handmaiden of the Divinity—of her willingness to let no-thing stand between her and the source of life. By declaring Mary to be the Mother of the Divinity, we acknowledge her as the source of the Divinity. And, finally, by her resurrection-assumption, we understand that, body and soul, she reigns beside her Son in glory. For us, it is a sign of what is to come. For the Divinity, it is a sign that the incarnated Feminine is now within the life of the Trinity itself.[65]

A second personal image of the Holy Spirit may be found in the biblical Wisdom literature in the one Kathleen O'Connor refers to as the Wisdom Woman.[66] Wisdom literature belongs within a broad international way of thinking and writing which includes Egyptians, Sumerians, Akkadians, Babylonians, Canaanites, and other major world religions such as Hinduism and Buddhism.[67] The starting point of Wisdom literature is human experience; the Wisdom Woman may be found in the marketplace.[68]

The way to enter into a relationship with Wisdom is not through prayer or piety, or through communal resolve or deciding, but by disciplined study (Wisdom 6:12 and 16).[69] "Disciplined study of all that comes into being (all that is created) results in a personal encounter with the One at the heart of the creative process."[70] What Wisdom teaches is not content; rather She is both teacher and that which is taught.[71] "The learning process is the way that humans share in the creative process."[72] In other words, we are called to be co-creators with Wisdom. Ultimately, it may be said that Wisdom is a divine gift, for while we may pursue Her, She is the one who finds us.[73]

A description of the Wisdom Woman as Divinity begins to emerge when we consider the following passages from scripture. Citing Proverbs 1:23, "Behold, I will pour out my thoughts to you; I will make my words known to you," O'Connor suggests that the promise of the Wisdom Woman to enter into a relationship with people in which She reveals all that She is, is a promise which in scripture is reserved for the Divinity alone.[74] Further, Sirach 24:3b-6—"Alone I made the circuit of the vault of heaven and walked in the depths of the abyss. In the waves of the sea, in the whole earth and in every people and nation I have gotten a possession"—describes activity that is reserved for the Divinity alone.[75] Likewise, Proverbs 8:33, "To find me is to find life," is a claim that only the Divinity could make.

The specific divine identification that the Wisdom Woman makes is with the Holy Spirit. This association of Spirit and Wisdom appears for the first time in Isaiah 40:13.[76] Spirit and Wisdom are further associated, for example, in Wisdom 1:1-15, a text used in the Roman Catholic liturgy of Pentecost.[77] And in Wisdom 7:22b-8:1, "the Old Testament theologies of wisdom and the spirit meet and are identified."[78] This identification of Wisdom and the Holy Spirit is again made explicit in Wisdom 9:17, "Who has learned thy counsel, unless thou has given wisdom and sent thy holy spirit from on high."[79] The Hebrew scriptures laid a strong foundation for the development of a theology on the Holy Spirit as Wisdom. That this did not happen may be termed a tragedy for our times when we are experiencing a world dominated by masculine values.[80] But it is not a tragedy that cannot be corrected; in fact, it is being corrected by all those who accept the invitation of Wisdom/the Holy Spirit to enter into relationship with Her.

The third personal image of the Holy Spirit is that of the feminine: as sister, as daughter, as mother, as friend. I find Her by going within where my own femininity can be a source of revelation concerning Her person. I find Her by going out where others may reveal to me who She is. I would say that there is something about my understanding of the feminine that interprets for me who the Holy Spirit is. However, She is more than the sum total of any woman, even Mary. She is more than the sum total of all women. She is not equated with some abstract philosophical concept such as the "eternal feminine." Nevertheless, I see in the Holy Spirit the supreme exemplification of what the feminine is. The issue then becomes one of defining what the feminine means. What are the appropriate images, words, symbols, experiences of the feminine? Does it, for example, encompass what we look at traditionally as feminine: gentleness, compassion, nurturance, and/or does it involve how we see the Holy Spirit in the Christian scriptures as very active and always "on the go"? This theologizing comes from my within—a within concerning the feminine Spirit that can only begin to form a whole when each of us—women and men—come together to explore who She is for us and for our Earth.

6.

The Feminine and the Major World Religions

In this age when it is no longer appropriate or possible to confine one's understanding to one's own religious heritage and practice, it seemed most appropriate to move out of my own Christian tradition and to look at the issue of the feminine in the other major "religions of the Book," Judaism and Islam. However, I also felt the need—the urging of the Spirit—to move beyond the religions of the Word and to touch what some refer to as the "creation religions." As Paul R. Fries has stated:

> A theology which cannot recognize God's presence and action apart from the Word revealed through Israel, the Messiah, or the church blinds itself to the Spirit of God in creation. The implications of such impaired vision are enormous. God's positive and significant presence and activity in "creation religions" (all but Judaism, Christianity and Islam) cannot be recognized, and thus dialogue remains impossible. ... Attempts to articulate an ecological ethic, urgently needed today, suffer from disconnection.[1]

My limiting myself to the other so-called major world religions—Hinduism, Judaism, Buddhism and Islam—is in no way intended to downplay the contributions, some of which have previously been referred to in this book, of the religions of the Great Goddess and the religions of the indigenous peoples. In fact, we are increasingly becoming aware of the contributions these traditions offer toward the healing of our present broken world. They are not included mainly because others, with far greater resources than I possess, are already hard at work in bringing their richness to our awareness.[2] In addition, all of the major world religions may be seen as a unit in that all are patriarchal; all are expressions of the culture in which they are rooted and which, all too often, they defend. But one area where they differ radically is in their expression—or lack thereof—of the

Feminine Ultimate. Thus, we find the many goddesses of Hinduism, the one God of Judaism and Islam, who is usually referred to as male, and the Buddhist's Absolute, which is without gender, but in whose antecedent, early Brahmanism, "we find a predominantly male pantheon and the rise of supreme [male] deities along with male social dominance."[3]

The relationship of these varied religions to the Feminine Ultimate and the light that this relationship sheds on women's and the Earth's issues will be undertaken in a chronological order: Hinduism, Judaism, Buddhism, and Islam. While the dating of Buddhism and Islam is rather straightforward—based on the dates of the lives of their founders, Gautama Siddhartha (c. 563-c. 483 B.C.E.) and Muhammad (570-632 C.E.) respectively, the beginning dates of Judaism and Hinduism are less apparent. I have settled upon the age of the patriarchs (Abraham: c. 1750? B.C.E.) for the beginning of what developed into present-day Judaism, and the flourishing of the Harappan culture, the ancestors of today's Dravidians (c. 3000 B.C.E.) for the beginning of what developed into contemporary Hinduism.[4] This choice of chronological age, rather than studying Buddhism after Hinduism, and Islam after Judaism—religions which are in close relationship and tension to one another—provides a unique focus for the relationship of the world's religions to the feminine as it developed in time. We turn now to Hinduism and its many goddesses to begin our study.

Hinduism—A Religion of Many Goddesses

For one who is coming out of a monotheistic tradition, the seemingly limitless number of goddesses and gods in the Hindu pantheon is overwhelming. Intellectually, it makes perfect sense when seen in a context that both affirms Oneness and the expression of that Oneness through the multitude of ways in which countless human beings have expressed their vision.[5] That vision may be expressed through a Deity regarded as she, he, or it, or a Deity who is beyond gender.[6] As a feminine expression of Deity, the Goddess has manifestations under the names of Candi (the fierce), Chamunda (the demon slayer), Annapurna (she of abundant food), Gauri (the golden one), Jagad Amba (world mother), Kulakalyayani (wisdom), Bhuvanesvari (earth), and Ambika (little mother)—to mention just a few.[7] Merlin Stone honors Her as "the thousand named Goddess, who sits upon the thousand petalled lotus of the cosmos, source of all energy, She who holds the entire universe in Her womb."[8]

For purposes of this study, we need not look at Her under Her "thousand" names. Rather, we will look at Her in relationship to the Feminine Principle, as the Great Goddess who is both Earth Mother and the cosmogonic principle, and as Durgā-Kali in Śākta Hinduism. We will conclude this section by looking at the worship of the Goddess as it relates to the status of women in India.

In the West, there seems to be a great deal of ambiguity and concern about the meaning of the term the *Feminine Principle*. In the East, for example, in the work of Vandana Shiva, the term seems to be used as a given. For our purposes, I offer the definition given by Tracy Pintchman, a Westerner writing on Hinduism, who characterizes the Feminine Principle in Vedic literature "as a kind of material emerging presence, a presence that both propels creation into being and also exists in embodied form as the physical cosmos."[9]

For Shiva, *Prakrti* is the manifestation of the Feminine Principle and is "characterized by (a) creativity, activity, productivity; (b) diversity in form and aspect; (c) connectedness and inter-relationship of all beings, including man [*sic*]; (d) continuity between the human and the natural; (e) sanctity of life in nature."[10] She contrasts this to the Cartesian world-view, where nature is our environment or resource, not our same substance. In this world-view, "nature is a) inert and passive; b) uniform and mechanistic; (c) separable and fragmented within itself; (d) separate from man [*sic*]; and (e) inferior, to be dominated and exploited by man."[11]

According to Pupul Jayakar, "an archaic peoples' culture based on the primacy of the feminine principle survived in secret women's rites and fertility rituals."[12] This is based on her understanding that modern Hinduism has carried much of its prehistory within itself. This occurred because its response to incursions—Aryans from around 1750 B.C.E., the persecutions of the Buddhists in the ninth and tenth centuries, the Muslim invasions between the eleventh and thirteen centuries—was one of retreats from the settled areas to the remote forests, villages, and mountains.[13] In these remote areas, this Divine Feminine Principle, when acting as protector and healer, is found as a composite of human, plant, and animal. In the transforming process, the animal part of Her takes on independent form and becomes Her vehicle. Likewise, the plant part of Her takes form as the lotus or other plants that surround Her.[14]

The oldest known female manifestation of the Feminine Principle is found in a bone image of the Mother, located in a cave in Mirzapur, Uttar Pradesh, and carbon dated at at least 20,000 B.C.E.[15] Hand-molded clay images of the Goddess at, for example, Mehrgarh in central Pakistan, are found in an unbroken line of succession lasting for eight thousand years, commencing in 6,000 B.C.E.[16] Jayakar describes this Goddess as linked "to energy, to the earth, and to manifestation."[17] This dark primordial Goddess was the Earth Mother who, as the Female Principle, encompassed both birth and death.[18] In death, there is both ending and the passage to a new beginning.[19] She was both mother and virgin, so no corresponding male principle was seen as necessary for society.[20] She images the tradition of woman as the original Creator, who has her origins in Adi Śakti, the first woman.[21] Geometrical abstractions were also employed to picture the Goddess and still are evidenced in the present-day worship at, for example, Bahuchara and Ambā. The earliest known example of this is the recent finding of a paleolithic shrine, expected to be dated at 10,000-8,000 B.C.E., in the Siddhi district of Madhya Pradesh.[22]

In time, numerous legends came into existence which told of the marriage of the Earth goddess to the Sun god, legends which symbolized the merging of the matriarchal culture (indigenous) with the patriarchal culture. Through their marriages and the loss of their virginal (independent) status, the Earth Mothers were tamed. The attendant male consorts, who were first protectors and guardians of the Earth Mothers, in time became gods in their own right.[23] An example of the ambiguous role the Goddess takes on when she is wedded to the patriarchal Aryan gods may be seen in the role assumed by Durgā, who performs the task of which the Brahmanic gods are incapable: slaying the black buffalo demon, Mahisa. Her role is ambiguous because, while on the one hand it is She, and not the gods, who is all-powerful, on the other hand, this power is used for their purposes. Furthermore, she is all light (Aryan?), while the buffalo demon represents the darkness (Dravidians?).[24]

The ambiguity is lessened when the association of the Earth with the Great Goddess is taken over by the male god Vishnu, that is, "the earth is described as belonging to Vishnu or as being the female principle in Vishnu in an embodied form—Bhur-vaishnavi."[25] Even less ambiguity exists when we read in the *Rig Veda* of the murder of the Mother Goddess, Danu, by the Aryan god Indra, or of the fate of the children of Diti, a name associated with the Mother Goddess of the Harappans. All of the children of Diti were slain, including the slaying by Indra of the embryo that She carried in her womb.[26]

But it was not only the Aryans who transformed the myths and lives of the autochthonous peoples; the conquerors were also transformed by those whom they conquered. Thus, Jayakar sees in the *Atharva Veda* "very archaic elements and . . . possibly the earliest record of the beliefs, the imagery, the rituals and worship of the autochthonous peoples of India as they met and transformed the conquering Aryan consciousness."[27] This transformation involved a shifting from the sky to the Earth—a shifting that expressed itself in concern for Mother Earth when the plow was used to lacerate her breast, a concern that called for propitiation, prayer, and healing.[28]

While the above is a positive reading of the Great Goddess as a manifestation of the Feminine Principle, an alternate reading is proposed by Lina Gupta. She chooses for her image Kali, who she says may be understood in either of two ways: "the mythic Great Mother whose symbolism depends on male fascination with female biology, or . . . the goddess who represents the ultimate principle of Hinduism that transcends any form of duality[?]."[29] Gupta argues that we must emphasize the second aspect if we are to move beyond patriarchy.[30] In a patriarchal and literal interpretation of scripture, Kali is seen as the female principle of *śakti* (raw unrestricted power), *prakrti* (unpredictable nature), *avidya* (ignorance or wrong knowledge) and *māyā* (trickery, deceit or illusion).[31] As part of a postpatriarchal interpretation, Gupta proposes Kali as warrior, the one who personifies the wrath that all women in all cultures experience. As warrior, she breaks through all boundaries by associating with animals and every life form no matter how lowly, through associating with the lowest members of the Hindu caste system, and through inhabiting the cremation ground where women, until recently, were not allowed to go because of their emotionality. As the wife of Śiva, while she may be tender and caring, she is also destructive and domineering—not at all conforming to the stereotypical ideal wife who is totally defined by her husband. In fact, further breaking the stereotype, Kali is usually found without a mate or husband at her side. While Indian law as codified by Manu (seventh century B.C.E.) decreed that a wife is to worship her husband as a god, Gupta says scripture sees both husband and wife as reflections of the Divine nature. (The One, Brahman, becomes dual: Śiva, male, and Śakti, female). However, at another level, Kali (Śakti) is Brahman, the all-inclusive Reality beyond all distinction.[32]

As well as being identified with the Earth, the Great Goddess is also seen as the cosmic force or principle. Jayakar speaks of Virāj whom she identifies with the female principle as a pervading cosmic force.[33] We read in the Hindu scriptures: "The earth was born from her [Virāj] who crouched with legs spread, and from the earth the quarters of the sky were born.[34] As cosmic principle, the theology of the Great Goddess (Mahādevi) is expounded within orthodox Brahmanical Hinduism in the *Purānas*, the vast mythological works dating from about the beginning of the fourth century C.E. to approximately the sixteenth century C.E.[35] She is Great/the Goddess because She "is identified with cosmogonic principles that are unique and transcend the particular identity of individual divinities."[36] These principles are: *śakti*, the power that begins the process of creation and sustains it; *prakrti*, the materiality which is the ground of all things; *māyā*, or illusion, which may be allied with either *śakti* or *prakrti*.[37] *Śākta* texts such as the *Devi-Bhāgavata* identify the Goddess as Nirguna Brahman or the Absolute.[38] While *śakti*, *māyā*, and *prakrti* are all feminine words, in earlier texts they are often not associated with a goddess nor are they equated with the Feminine Principle. These relationships come about when the older texts are reworked in conjunction with a newer type of literature, that is, the mythological. Pintchman contends that through the reworking of the creation myths and cosmological motifs, Brahmanical orthodoxy was maintained by employing the time-honored principles of *śakti*, *māyā*, and *prakrti*, but the end result, the elevation of the Feminine Principle to supreme status, was basically non-Brahmanical.[39]

Shiva also speaks in terms of the Feminine Creative Principle of the cosmos—the source of all existence—which she identifies as *Śakti*. According to Shiva, *Prakrti* is how the power of *Śakti* is manifested, that is, *Prakrti* is the power of nature, both animate and inanimate. As such, nature is seen as dynamic energy.[40] *Prakrti* is further identified as "the Mother of

Nature who is nature itself born of the creative play of her thought."[41] Hers is the will to become the many; diversity; the abundance of Creation. *Prakrti inhabits* each part of creation; therefore, a mountain, for example, is dynamic.[42]

The Goddess is also the concern of Wendell Charles Beane in his study on *Śākta* Hinduism—the Hinduism of the villages and "little" people—which is characterized by more deities who are distinctly feminine, in contrast to the Great Tradition, whose pantheon of gods is more masculine.[43] Beane sees *Śakti* (female power/energy) as a unifying symbol of "both the non-Sanskritic, popular, and exoteric and the Sanskritic, philosophical, and esoteric ... traditions."[44] While the Goddess is rooted in the worship of the Earth Mother, She ultimately becomes the new Creatrix, replacing Brahmā in the Indian *trimurti*.[45] She is both transcendent and immanent. As transcendent, She has an Ultimate Form which is Formlessness. She is the Abyss of Power as Transcendental Form whom even the gods cannot know unless She so chooses. As immanent (intimate), She is known to her devotees in a concrete human female form, a form related to her ultimate form, which is the Macro-anthropic Feminine.[46] The dissolution of the universe(s) occurs if the Goddess—who is both the Mother of time and the Destroyer of time—closes her eyes. Such an action not only dissolves the universe(s), but also the great gods such as Brahmā, Shiva, and Vishnu, who are "ultimately understood to be merely *instrumental* to the eternal Play (*Lila*) of the goddess whom they, too, worship."[47] Beane characterizes the Goddess as the one who can say "I do whatever I wish," a statement of ontological independence which he compares to Exodus 33:19 and Romans 9:15ff. When manifested as Umā, She is the One who is needed to reveal to both the gods and humans who Brahman is; as such, She is Ultimate knowledge, permanent salvation.[48] She is needed to transform the chaos into Cosmos; the gods all fail; only She who is Absolute Power (Śakti) is capable of performing this task. In Indra's inability to restore the cosmos—to re-create—is symbolized the passing of the old martial order and "the birth of a new reverence, power, and harmony now in the hands of the Eternal Goddess."[49] The Universe itself is omni-sacred because there is nothing in it that is not filled with the presence of the Goddess as Creatrix.[50]

In *Śākta* Hinduism, the Śakti-Śiva symbol is the cosmic personification of Brahman, the mascroscopic Impersonal. It may be characterized as a symbol of diadic univalence, that is, a mutual reality in which the identity, power, and activity of the two Primary Ultimates (Śiva and Śakti) enjoy interchangeability of identify, power, and activity. As such, they symbolize the "creative process of Being and Becoming, Cause and Effect, Power-Holding and Power-Holder. ... Their ultimate (actual) unity remains structurally inseparable from their intimate (potential) disunity as a reflection of sensuous-spatial human experience."[51] Śiva and Śakti are each benevolent and malevolent in character. In the Śakti-Śiva symbolism is found the "cosmogonic *metasexual* prototype of the process of mundane procreation."[52]

> The goddess, then, like Śiva (Naṭarāja) can also be conceived as the Great Feminine Player: in Creation, Preservation, *and* Destruction (*vide infra*). Her movements can thus be seen in structural-symbolic unity with Śiva's; she is to be understood as his dynamic form, the kinetic aspect of Śiva as the static (passive) transcendental principle of the universe; but, then, this passivity of Śiva constitutes *no real or permanent duality*, because in essence the goddess is *his* activity and Śiva's passivity is *her* inactivity.[53]

The above has presented the Hindu Feminine Ultimate—as Feminine Principle, as Earth Mother, as cosmogonic principle, as Great Goddess—as a powerful symbol. What still remains to be discussed is how this Feminine Ultimate affects the actual lives of those who worship Her. Reading backward, Jayakar cites a line from the *Mahābhārata* as evidence that the women of pre-epic India enjoyed a freer existence that they lost when "the germ of male supremacy inherent in the Aryan creed had established itself."[54] Even today, this link to the time when women were priestesses and seers who guarded the mysteries survives in the rural areas in the form of *vratas*—rituals, homeopathic magic, and alchemy.[55]

The transition time when women moved from their "freer existence" to their present-day status may also be found by "reading between the lines" in the *Mahābhārata*. The taming of the Earth Mothers through their marriages to the Aryan gods and the subsequent loss of their virginal (independent) status, may also be the legendary recounting of the experiences of the real life indigenous women.[56] Gupta also addresses this transitional period—and the present—and finds "that patriarchal understanding has appropriated the goddesses and the feminine aspects of the Ultimate Reality at the heart of Hinduism in ways that sanction the unequal treatment of women."[57] In addition to the myths, Gupta cites the Hindu law codified by Manu in the seventh century B.C.E. as evidence for the severe limitation of the freedom of women. According to this law, women were defined solely as daughter, wife, and mother, and labeled as of a treacherous nature.[58]

However, there were (are) areas of India relatively unaffected by the Aryan invaders. These include the Malabar coast of the southwest, where the social structure was recorded as matrifocal and matrilineal and polyandry was practiced. Women poets also flourished here. Here the *Ammas*—the Mothers—are still worshipped. A second area worth noting—in the northeast—includes Bengal and Assam. Here matrifocal and matrilineal customs still exist, and women are found in the highest ranks of the Tantric Yoga clergy. It is here that people first spoke out against the custom of suttee or widow burning. Caste discrimination is discouraged as well, with "pride in family" and "pride in caste" considered obstacles to enlightenment. The Goddess is worshipped as Kali, Candi, Chamunda, and Śakti.[59]

It is not only women, but men also, who are involved in the worship of the Great Goddess. However, this worship has not always worked for women's benefit as men sometimes fear re-engulfment or become so fixated on Her that they project their fears onto women. Thus, on the religious plane, they adore the Great Goddess, while on the human plane, they are misogynists.[60] This dichotomy between male worship of the Goddess within Tantric Hinduism and the treatment of women is also noted by Beane. While within the religious sphere, woman is seen as the living embodiment of the Goddess, that is, as Power which is Creative and Ultimate, within Hindu society she is seen as the "modest spouse, as exemplified by Hindu goddesses such as Laksmī, Parvatī, and Umā. This may be at least partially explained as the failure of the myth itself, that is, as well as a Śakti-Śiva myth of mutuality, there is also the understanding of duality as dominance—the Goddess as the All. Beane thinks this frightens the male.[61] While this may lead us to the valid conclusion that we all—Hindu and non-Hindu alike—need to work to develop our myths of mutuality, as well as the living out of these myths in our everyday lives, we are still left with the dilemma of how to do this in a society that is asymmetrical. We might begin by seeing the female sex, whether plant, animal, or human, as a type of the Great Goddess and therefore deserving of reverence.[62]

Judaism—The Feminine in a Monotheistic Context

The monotheistic tradition which is equated so strongly with Judaism appears to leave little space for the honoring of the Feminine Divine. However, both feminists within that tradition—and some men who recognize their own need for the Feminine Divine—are looking today for ways in which that symbol may be honored. Thus, Raphael Patai turns to the study of comparative religion, which he says teaches us that there has always existed within man [sic] a need for the Feminine Divine as great, or even greater than, the need for a Masculine Divine symbol.[63] He argues that the Feminine Divine has occurred alongside official Hebrew monotheism in several forms throughout its history: in the goddesses Asherah, Astarte, and Anath, from the time of the Canaanite conquest until the Babylonian exile; as the female Cherubs found, for example, in the Second Temple; as the *Shekhina* or Divine Presence; as the Matronit (Matron, Lady, or Queen) of the Kabbala. This understanding of the Divine as feminine came full circle when, in the sixteenth century C.E., in the work of Moses Cordovera, a Kabbalist, the Matronit—Shekhina—is identified with Asherah.[64] For his evidence that the Divine was worshiped as feminine alongside the masculine Yahweh, Patai relies largely on the Hebrew scriptures, citing, for example, Jeremiah 44:15-19. In this passage, the people interpret their exile as a punishment for stopping their worship of the Queen of Heaven (Astarte-

Anath?); they contend that all was well for them when they worshiped Her and that they will resume that worship while in exile.[65] Patai also cites recent archeological evidence that includes three inscriptions (two in the Sinai and one near Hebron) which refer to Yahweh and his Asherah; this seems to indicate that Asherah was regarded as the consort of Yahweh.[66]

Also reinterpreting Hebrew scripture, but with concern for the role of the matriarchs rather than the Feminine Divine, is the writing of Savina J. Teubal. She places her work on the matriarchs within the context of what we have learned recently about the ancient Near East from the archeological and written records from the time of the matriarchs and patriarchs. Her writing explains the episodes in Sarah's life from the perspective of her being a priestess, a representative of a goddess. The episodes explained include Sarah's being given to Pharaoh and King Abimelech; her barrenness; her giving of her handmaiden to Abraham so that she may have children through her; her supernatural conception of Isaac; her conflict with Hagar and Ishmael; her burial.[67] Thus, for example, the issue of Sarah's barrenness may be explained by her being a priestess of a goddess, and as such, virtually bound to childlessness. This would also apply to Rebekah and Rachel; it offers a plausible explanation for the unlikely occurrence that three generations of matriarchs would be afflicted by "barrenness."[68] As priestess, Sarah is a woman of authority who represents an alternative system to patriarchy; she also represents a role model for present-day Jewish women who struggle, as she did, against a patriarchal system.[69]

During the Hellenistic period, the image of Sophia, the Feminine Divine Wisdom, came into prominence because Israel needed such a mythic figure to enable it to respond to the problems presented to it by its social setting — a setting for which its other images failed to provide adequate responses. "While groups within the priestly tradition in Israel and Judaism sought to separate and re-isolate the Hebrew faith, the wisdom tradition was trying to integrate the Hebrew perspective into the larger picture."[70] One such connection may be seen in the Hebrew understanding of Wisdom and the Egyptian understanding of the goddess Maat. Both may be seen as order, truth, justice, and the Feminine Divinity personified; the thought of the Creator's heart; "his" companion; the very life of the universe; giver of the Law; coming from heaven in the beginning and making their dwelling with earthlings; the principle Divine power; the foundation and the former of social and cosmic life.[71] As a symbol addressing today's needs, Sophia, as both created and Creator, provides an image of what it means to be co-creator with the Divinity. She also breaks the stereotype of transcendence being equated with God-male and immanence with Earth-female; rather, Sophia is experienced as transcendence and equated with Heaven-female. Because She represents a female religious symbol system, She enables women to claim power as their right.[72]

In post-biblical times, the Feminine Divine is most apparent in Jewish mysticism, specifically in Kabbalism and Hasidism. There we find anthropomorphized the one Godhead as the Holy One, Blessed be He, and the *Shekhina*. According to Patai, this was its great weakness from a theological point of view—given the difficulty this would present in a religion that was strictly monotheistic. At the same time, this was also its great strength from a psychological point of view—given the necessity for the male [*sic*] to be in touch with the Feminine Divine.[73] The prayer for unification of God and His *Shekhina* is even today part of the ritual of Hasidic Ashkenazi, Sephardi, and Oriental Jewish communities.[74] However, one may ask if, in fact, this use does not raise the issue of the possible use of an inferior Feminine Divine symbol to keep historical women in a comparable inferior place?

Before turning to the modern Jewish feminist response to the issues they see raised by their tradition, I would like to summarize the above with a quotation from Patai:

> What ultimately emerges from this conspectus is that, contrary to the generally held view, the religion of the Hebrews and the Jews was never without at least a hint of the feminine in its God-concept. At times, as in the Talmudic and even more so in the post-Talmudic periods, the female element in the deity was effectively pushed into the background. At others, as in the Biblical and again in the Kabbalistic eras, it occupied an important place in popular theology, occasionally even to the extent of overshadowing the male deity or the male component of the godhead. Only in the most recent times, after the Kabbalistic upsurge had subsided, and its last reverberations in Hasidism receded, was the female element eliminated from the God-concept among Reform, Conservative, and non-Hasidic Orthodox Jews, leaving it centered upon a strictly spiritual, but nevertheless inescapably masculine godhead, upon "our Father in heaven." On the other hand, among the Sephardim, the Oriental Jews, and the Hasidic Ashkenazim, despite the inroads modernism has begun to make in their ranks, the mystical-mythical doctrine of God and the Shekhina has retained its hold, not in the least due to the fact that in these circles the reverence for the teachings of old Kabbalistic, respectively Hasidic, masters is still a powerful influence.[75]

Susannah Heschel sees feminism as a major revision of Judaism, comparable to the shift from a sacrificial to a liturgical system that resulted from the destruction of the Temple. She notes that increasing numbers of Jewish feminists insist that women will cease being "other" and become normative only when there is a shift in the language and imaging of the Divinity to include the feminine as She or Goddess.[76]

For Judith Plaskow also, the reform that is needed in Judaism is one that will deal with the "otherness" of women and the fact that their religious experiences are absent from the whole of the tradition and its formulation.

She sees the need for incorporating these experiences in Torah and in Israel (community) and the imaging of God [*sic*] as well. Plaskow specifically notes that reform of the Torah will not bring about the needed changes for women within Judaism because it does not go to the root causes of the problem; in fact, the Law is a symptom of the problem rather than its cause. She cites the absence of the full equality of women in Reform Judaism as a concrete example that shows that the issue is not the Law.[77] Rather, for Plaskow, new metaphors of God must be capable of evoking the Divine Presence in the community of Israel where that community is characterized as empowered, egalitarian, and diverse. God as male and as dominating Other would not fulfill these criteria.[78] In regard to God as male, Plaskow argues that male language has become an idol in the Jewish community. Even Maimonides was apparently not conscious, in applying his theology of negation to the Divinity, that he did not treat maleness as an attribute, but rather accepted the fact that God was male![79] In regard to God as dominating Other, female imagery in itself does not address the problem.[80] In other words, the female, as well as the male, can be dominating. In seeking the non-dominating Feminine Divine, Plaskow turns to pronouns, to the tradition, and to new images. In the tradition, she discusses the image of the *Shekhina*. This image offers the advantages of already being a part of the tradition; of being an image of Divine immanence, an image of relationship rather than the Divine as dominating Other. On the negative side, this image comes out of a male tradition, is a male understanding of the feminine, and the subordinate consort of the masculine God.[81] Turning to new images for the Divine, possible sources are the Native American traditions, the Goddess, nature, and the human as part of the web of life.[82] Personal images which are more suggestive of the God of the covenant than king and lord include lover, friend, co-creator, and companion. As well as personal images, Plaskow also suggests impersonal images — ground of life, source, rock, tree, light and darkness — which draw us from heaven to the Earth.[83] The Goddess, whom Plaskow defines as "God-She, but in a clearer and more powerful way,"[84] leads Plaskow to confront the issue of "paganism." She finds the Jewish contempt of paganism to be comparable to Christian anti-Semitism. This comparison is based on the parallel that she finds in both sets of scriptures: in the Hebrew scriptures, against the Canaanites and a religion that had sustained them for millennia; in the Christian scriptures, against the Jews and a religion that had likewise sustained them for millennia. The charge of "paganism" is, in this light, not one that feminists need to take seriously. Rather, they need to affirm a monotheism that is all-inclusive, including the feminine.[85] In summary, Plaskow argues that we can still retain the Otherness of God while leaving behind the idea of domination. Otherness is seen in the fact that God is more than the sum of all that is; metaphors for God encompass that which is often despised such as femaleness, darkness, nature; God is ultimately mystery, enemy as well as friend, somehow the source of evil, death, pain, and decay.[86]

Rita Gross has also addressed the issue of God-language using the foci of pronouns and new images. Thus, for example, she finds "the Holy One, blessed be She" to be as appropriate as "the Holy One, blessed be He."[87] Regarding feminine images of the Deity, these might include: "the coincidence of opposites" (death and birth, darkness and light); female sexuality; the feminine as non-stereotypical (strong, trustworthy); as mother and cultural symbol. Their importance lies in the fact that, by breaking stereotypes, the Goddess frees women themselves from these stereotypes; for example, women can be both strong and beautiful. Second, Goddess images restore the lost dimensions of immanence, acceptance, nature, and cyclic round, and bring wholeness to the partial truths of transcendence, intervention, history, and linear time.[88]

Jewish feminists looking to their own traditions are finding them a resource, not only for theologizing, but also for ritualizing. Thus, the *Shekhina* as the Tabernacle of Peace is recalled by women in the lighting of the Sabbath candles, re-enacting the idea of the universe as macrocosm-microcism. "Because the Tabernacle of Peace the [*Shekhinah*] rests on us during the Sabbath, on the [Sabbath -] souls, it is therefore proper for us to do below, in this form, as it is done above [within the Godhead], to kindle the lights."[89] As well as the Sabbath, Rosh Hodesh, the monthly holiday marking the new moon, "has become a woman's way to apprehend the *Shekhina*, the Divine Presence in this world"; thus, the Jewish calendar itself "becomes a vehicle for noting the monthly cycles of women's fertility and understanding the female aspects of God."[90] A third example is the use of minor holidays such as Tu B'shivat. Ellen Bernstein turns this minor holiday, which honors trees, into a major environmental holy day, which takes into account our larger responsibility to nature as a whole.[91]

Women's religious experience includes not only symbols and ritual, but also the use of the imagination. Thus, Carol Christ suggests that, by changing places with God [*sic*], women may discover that God is a woman who has had Her identity stolen by the patriarchy. She sees the need for a new covenant that would liberate women, God, and our sister the Earth, whom the Divinity once represented.[92] This issue of the use of the imagination is also taken up by Naomi Goldenberg, but from a post-Judaic perspective. However, before proceeding to the insights of Goldenberg, we need to look at a final Jewish feminist reformer who offers an alternate proposal to those cited above.

Cynthia Ozick questions the thesis that the lack of self-esteem among Jewish women should be responded to by looking at the lack of the feminine in the concept of the deity.[93] Rather, she sees the issue as a question of justice of scandalous proportions. The solution is to strengthen the Torah itself through a commandment which forbids the dehumanizing of woman — a change in Torah which she finds comparable and as necessary as the change which took place after the destruction of the Second Temple – an event which called into question the Torah itself.[94] Looking also at the issue of law (*kashrut* or dietary laws), Plaskow finds a system already in place that reminds one of the sanctity of animal life. She suggests the extension of this sanctity to one of full vegetarianism; or alternatively, the eating of no foods that contain pesticides, carcinogens, or hormones.[95]

In the fall of the patriarchal religions – specifically Judaism and Christianity – Goldenberg sees "a chance to experiment with more democratic forms of religiosity."[96] With their fall, we no longer have to limit ourselves to transcendent, perfect ideals which negated certain races, the female sex, and parts of our own bodies. To move in this new direction, she suggests that we give our own images the standing of archetypes. Despite the individuality that this would call forth, community could still be created, but it would be community based on a shared process involving our imaging rather than on a shared content involving only certain archetypes.[97] One image that many women are articulating is that of the Goddess of feminist witchcraft, an image that is concrete and many-faceted.[98] In witchcraft, Goldenberg finds "the first modern theistic religion to conceive of its deity mainly as an internal set of images and attitudes."[99] As well as witchcraft, she sees the future of religion in the West based in mysticism "which emphasizes the *continual observation of psychic imagery*."[100] This mysticism of the psychoreligious age will be post-Judaic and post-Christian.[101] Goldenberg sees image and life as intimately related, so that we see not only the imaginal aspects of tangible things, but even more important, "*the tangible aspects of imaginal things.*"[102] Dreams are a way to move into our interior spaces and discover these images, which are all parts of ourselves.[103]

In summary, it may be said that Jewish feminism is just beginning to create a "new way of being" for Judaism. This new way of being calls for *Tikkun olam* – the right ordering of society. This involves many dimensions, but includes the cosmic dimension, that is, the embracing of all parts of the world as embodying the Sacred Presence,[104] and the personal dimension, valuing of our bodies, which also leads to valuing the Earth of which our bodies are part. In so doing, we would address the issues of environmental pollution, toxic wastes, poisoning of the food supply, and so forth, and the issues of the poor, who look not to fullness of life but to survival.[105] Whether the Jewish community will accept this challenge, as it accepted the challenge presented by the destruction of the Second Temple, it is too early to know. But may it be so.

Buddhism – The Feminine in a Non-theistic Context

In Buddhism, it is truly possible to state that the Absolute Reality is without gender. This follows from Buddhism's rejection of all dualities, including that of gender. However, if we look to its antecedent, early Brahmanism, we find "a predominantly male pantheon and the rise of supreme [male] deities along with male social dominance."[106] This context, into which Buddhism was born, may at least in part account for the fact that Buddhism is not free of sexism. But just as early Brahmanism influenced Buddhism at its formative stages, there are other influences on it today. Thus, Buddhism on the North American continent may be characterized as a new vehicle that "is being deeply affected by the spirit of democracy, by feminization, by ecological values, and by the integration of lay life."[107] Of the above mentioned areas of impact, feminization may be the most important element, as evidenced not only in the abandonment of the structures of sexism and patriarchy, but also as "a more profound movement to develop the *Dharma* as a practice of relationship to the body, the community, and the earth, and to stress interdependence and healing rather than conquering or abandoning."[108] But before looking at some of the ways in which Buddhism and feminism have interacted in our time, we will look at some key texts of Buddhism in order to glean some understanding of the status of women in this tradition.

Based on her readings of *Mahāyāna* literature, Diana Paul sets forth two cross-cultural themes in regard to the feminine and women's status in Buddhist society. The first theme is the depiction of the feminine as "mysterious, sensual, destructive, elusive, and closer to nature"; the second theme is the depiction of the feminine as "wise, maternal, creative, gentle, and compassionate."[109] In the first instance, women are generally perceived as threatening to men; in the second instance, they are generally seen as necessary to the achievement of men's religious goals. The threatening element is shown, for example, in a myth that depicts the Earth as feminine. The myth, found in the *Aganna-suttanta* text of the *Pāli* canon, speaks of a Golden Age and a fall from this age. In the myth there exists a relationship between the devolution of the once heavenly, asexual, noncorporeal and self-illuminated beings and the feminine Earth; that is, their devolution begins when one of the beings tastes the Earth and the others follow this example.[110] However, women's role in regard to other women's spiritual well-being is rarely mentioned in the scriptures. Furthermore, the relationship between ultimate spiritual perfection (Buddhahood) and the feminine is viewed with ambivalence by Buddhist scholars and commentators. The ambiguity exists because of the principle of equality toward both sexes based on the teaching of Emptiness and the discrimination toward women which exists in reality. Thus, all the Buddhas in the *Mahāyāna* sutra literature are portrayed as male, androgynous, or asexual, with the male portrayals being predominate. The relationship between a male Divine Principle and a female Divine Principle is not explored in *Mahāyāna* Buddhism; the issue is, however, explored in *Tantricism*.[111] Paul summarizes this situation as follows:

The inconsistency in beliefs and values is readily apparent in maintaining the elimination of sexuality as essential to Buddhahood, but

adhering to masculinity as the ideal state rather than to one of asexuality. By definition, feminine images of Buddhahood are a contradiction in terms if asexuality denotes the masculine state.[112]

An examination of the issue of whether or not women can attain enlightenment as women will be undertaken by looking at the role of the *Bodhisattva* — the role of one who is destined for future Buddhahood but
postpones the attainment of Nirvana in order to teach and comfort all
beings, not only the human. The role of the *Bodhisattva* is one to which
all — female and male — may aspire. Paul classifies the female's role as
regards becoming a *Bodhisattva* in the *Mahāyāna* tradition into three categories. The first denies the possibility of a woman entering Pure Land;
the second, which contains the majority of the literature, accepts women
as lower stage *Bodhisattvas*; the third genre addresses the issue of women
as advanced *Bodhisattvas*, that is, imminent Buddhas. In regard to the first
genre, it may be said that probably the best that women can do in the
current life is hope to be reborn a male in the next rebirth.[113] The second
stage, where women are relegated to a lower stage of spiritual development
than their male counterparts, reflects "both the social order of India at
that time and the monastic hierarchical structure of the community wherein
even the most senior nun must be deferential to the youngest novice
monk."[114] While this reflects the majority of the *sutra* literature (the discourses believed to be the words of the Buddha), an interesting exception
occurs when a woman's virtues and merits are so exceptional that they must
be treated as such (genre 3). In such cases, one response is to make the
attainment of *Bodhisattvahood* and even Buddhahood possible by calling
for a transformation of sex from female to male.[115] Thus, for example, "the
goddess of the Ganges," an excerpt from one of the oldest *Mahāyāna sutras*,
shows the Buddha predicting the goddess's sexual transformation in her
next rebirth with her residing in the Buddha land of *Aksobhya*. In a later
text, "The Nāga Princess," the sexual change occurs in this lifetime after
the prediction of Buddhahood has been given. This order of events is
retained in the story of the girl Candrottara, but in the story of the Daughter
Sumati, the prediction is not given until after the sexual transformation
from female to male in this life. This transformation, according to Paul,
symbolizes a more advanced stage of spiritual development.[116]

Even more interesting are the stories which speak of female *Bodhisattvas*
who do not undergo sexual transformation. One may argue that, if all is
illusion, there is no such thing as maleness or femaleness, and sexual transformation is therefore meaningless. (Texts which argue thusly form but a
small part of the *Mahāyāna* scripture.) From *The Sutra of the Teaching of
Vimalakirti*, Paul presents two episodes. In the first story, the enlightened
female companions of *Māra*, the evil one, are urged to return to him and
convert others from within the existing social system. In the second presentation, a goddess, whose name is not given, argues from a philosophical

position on the absurdity of holding that there is innate distinction among phenomena. And, finally, in the story of the *Bodhisattva* Jewel Brocade, we find her refusing to abandon her femaleness and arguing persuasively that there is no place in the Buddha's teachings for such distinctions. The Buddha honors her position, and says she will attain Buddhahood and be known as Universal World.[117] *The Sutra of Queen Śrīmālā Who had the Lion's Roar* perhaps best exemplifies the issue of the unanswered nature of the question of whether or not women were ever recognized as potential or imminent Buddhas—for if in fact her Buddhahood is accepted as imminent (a debated question), it is still unclear whether the queen is a female *Bodhisattva* or a male *Bodhisattva* in female appearance.[118]

In *Mahāyāna* Buddhism, there also are feminine figures who were (are) worshiped in India, China, Tibet, and Japan. Some *Bodhisattvas* were deified beginning in fifth-century India. Since the celestial *Bodhisattvas* were renowned for their mercy and compassion, it was only natural that people who were in need of mercy and compassion would turn to them in times of need. For our purposes, the most interesting celestial *Bodhisattva* is Avalokiteśvara (Kuan-yin), statues of whom were common in India by the fifth century. While Kuan-yin is represented as male in India, in China Kuan-yin is usually represented as female.[119] The introduction of the celestial feminine *Bodhisattva* into *Mahāyāna* Buddhism by the late fourth century radically separated it from the earlier *Theravādin* tradition "in which the Buddha was the father figure without an accompanying mother figure."[120] While there is some extremely sparse evidence in India that Avalokiteśvara existed as the feminine Avalokitā (the state of looking down), in China in the seventh and early eighth centuries, the predominant portrayal of Kuan-yin is as a delicate, slender, white-clad female. This Goddess of Mercy became known in Japan as Kannon, where, as in China, she was the patroness of women desiring children and sailors seeking protection from the disasters associated with the seas. The earliest scriptural references to Kuan-yin as female occur in the Chinese translation of the *Lotus Sutra* from 406 C.E., where seven of the thirty-three appearances show her as female.[121] Today Kuan-yin is regarded by many as the Universal Principle of salvation[122]; she gives to all the light of Wisdom, in which instance She is sometimes depicted with one thousand hands and one thousand eyes.[123]

In Tibetan Buddhism, Wisdom also has an honored place. There we find Prajñāpāramitā, the Perfection of Wisdom, who is called the mother of all the Buddhas. She is first explicated in *Perfection of Wisdom in Eight Thousand Lines*, dated in the late second and first centuries B.C.E.[124] Prajñāpāramitā represents a new archetype of the Feminine Principle, one that is no longer bound to the chthonic, but rather displays characteristics such as light, space, emptiness, and an all-encompassing gaze which is "both clinical and compassionate."[125] In the attribute of space, however, she is not set in opposition to the Earth, but is rather seen as the ground of being. This linkage of Wisdom to the Earth may be seen specifically in the Buddha's calling upon her as his witness to his act of enlightenment. In so doing, "he reached down, touched her, to affirm his right to be there and to destroy Māra's [the Evil One's] illusions."[126] In regard to the World, Prajñāpāramitā calls one, not to the safety of Nirvana, but to full engagement with this side of reality, an engagement undertaken by the *Bodhisattva* for the sake of all beings.[127] Joanna Macy links the taking hold of this concept of the feminine in Tibetan soil with the fact that they are a nomadic people who gave the females of their society a dignity and freedom unknown in the agricultural society of North India.[128]

In the Tibetan tradition is also found the Green Tara, whose color symbolized her power to take action for countless beings. Tara is also seen as embodying the feminine presence in the world, a presence where there is "no separation between the one who suffers and the one who responds."[129] In an interview, the Dalai Lama asserted that Tara may be seen as a strong feminist for, despite the lack of role models, she insisted that she would receive enlightenment while retaining her female form. And she did.[130]

The power to develop the Feminine Principle is also found in Tibetan Buddhism, where it is a very traditional and important practice. The principle is called *Vajrayogini* and is known as "the glorious co-emergent Mother." Through this practice, appreciation and awareness of the Feminine Principle in the world and in the self is developed in both women and men.[131] Rita Gross holds that it is necessary that the masculine and feminine principles be held in balance by both sexes. She sees balance as involving "strength, independence, interdependence, complementarity and co-equality."[132] Through Buddhist practice, "feminine" concepts, which are regarded in the West with negativity, such as space and wisdom, can become positive forms of energy. While Gross does not regard women as more feminine than men, she does find that developing a special relationship with *Vajrayogini* held special significance for her as a Western woman who had grown up with no positive female role models.[133]

While environmental concerns are addressed peripherally in the above, one present-day Buddhist ecofeminist, Stephanie Kaza, has addressed this issue explicitly through the development of six "environmentally-relevant principles" wherein Buddhist and feminist principles overlap and complement one another. First, both Buddhism and feminism value experiential knowing over abstract other-generated ways of knowing; this embodied way of knowing grounds one in reality as it actually is, rather than in an ideal of reality. From this grounding, one is able to speak out and act on environmentally sensitive issues. Second, both understand the necessity to break through the thought patterns which have conditioned our minds. These include the thought patterns of stereotyping of animals and ecosystems; of projections in which reality is reduced to one's own ideas; of dualistic thinking. Kaza sees a lack in Buddhism in this area which may be traced to its transmission in a patriarchal culture. Third, both see interrelatedness or mutual becoming as a core truth. For the Buddhist, one powerful image is the Jewel Net of Indra, which encourages the human component of the Net to act in an ethically valuable way toward other members of the Net. For the ecofeminist, one example of this interrelatedness is seen in the development of an ethics of care and responsibility. Fourth, both recognize the importance of emotional response to the environmental crisis. By enabling a person to deal in depth with his or her emotions, Buddhist practice frees one for responsive action on behalf of the environment. For the feminist, emotions such as anger can provide the energy to respond morally to environmental degradation. However, Kaza cautions us that our emotional responses need to be deep and fully informed, lest they simply become obstacles for the healing that must occur. Fifth, both are grounded in an ethics of relationality. Key to *Mahāyāna* tradition and feminist experience is the practice of compassion. Buddhism and feminism both see the need to contextualize ethics rather than to see issues from a rights, rules, and abstract principles perception. Sixth, both understand the critical role that community plays. For example, Buddhists may consider themselves to be members of an ecocommunity (*Sangha*) in which all the nonhuman members are also participants; feminists may also understand the need for community as the place where we learn to redefine our relationship with one another and with the surrounding bioregion.[134]

I close this section by citing a project on the life of Buddha which depicts his life in such a way as to demonstrate his consciousness and concern for the environment. Through slides and narrative, Chatsumarn Kabilsingh has developed a presentation which she hopes will inspire other Buddhists to imitate his example.[135] It is hoped that her work is the beginning of heightened Buddhist consciousness on environmental issues in Southeast Asia.

Islam—Women's Challenge from within the Tradition

While it is officially said that the God of Islam has no gender, this would seem to be denied by the fact that Allah is referred to as he and not as she. The reality of the nature of God may be more truly found in the statement of Nawal el Saadawi:

> The oppression of women is not essentially due to particular religious ideologies. The great religions of the world (of both East and West) uphold similar principles as far as the submission of women to men is concerned. *They also agree in the attribution of masculine characteristics to God* [italics added].[136]

There seem to be few instances within the tradition where theologians have addressed the issue of the feminine dimension of the Divine. One theologian who did is Ibn al-ᶜArabi, who lived in the twelfth and thirteenth centuries. He saw the Feminine Divine as Wisdom and as the creative

Breath of Mercy. He also used Adam and Eve, and Mary and Jesus, to
argue for complementarity of the sexes.[137] Al-ᶜArabi also "discovered that
the word *dhāt*, 'essence,' is feminine and thus gained a feminine aspect for
the inner life of the deity."[138] As today's Islamic women receive training in
theology, we can look forward to more theologizing of the kind found in
the writings of al-ᶜArabi. These, apparently, are now sparse. What does
exist is writings by Islamic women who are looking at the situation of women
at the time Muhammad received his revelations, at the time of transition
to present-day Islam, and at the present status of Islamic women. It is to
these writings that the remainder of this section will be devoted.

Leila Ahmed finds that the Islamists' (those who advocate veiling) argument which states that the banning of infanticide improved women's position in all respects is both simplistic and inaccurate. Rather, she contends
that in Arabia, before Islam, women enjoyed greater sexual autonomy and
participated and were in fact leaders in a greater range of activities including religion and warfare. She uses the example of two of Muhammad's
wives to illustrate her point. In his first wife, Khadija, we find a wealthy
woman who employed Muhammad to help run her caravan business and
who proposed marriage to him. Though she was fifteen years his senior,
she remained his only wife until her death about twenty-five years later.
For his wife 'Aisha, in a marriage which was contracted after Muhammad
was recognized as a prophet and the leader of Islam, neither autonomy nor
monogamy any longer existed.[139] On a broader scale, Ahmed describes the
women of Arabia before Islam and at the transition to Islam in the following
terms:

> Jahilia women were priests, soothsayers, prophets, participants in war-
> fare, and nurses on the battlefield. They were fearlessly outspoken,
> defiant critics of men; authors of satirical verse aimed at formidable
> male opponents; keepers, in some unclear capacity, of the keys of the
> holiest shrine in Mecca; rebels and leaders of rebellions that included
> men; and individuals who initiated and terminated marriages at will,
> protested the limits Islam imposed on that freedom, and mingled-
> freely with the men of the society until Islam banned such interaction.
>
> In transferring rights to women's sexuality and their offspring from
> the woman and her tribe to men and then basing the new definition
> of marriage on that proprietary male right, Islam placed relations
> between the sexes on a new footing. Implicit in this new order was
> the male right to control women and to interdict their interactions
> with other men. Thus the ground was prepared for the closures that
> would follow: women's exclusion from social activities in which they
> might have contact with men other than those with rights to their
> sexuality; their physical seclusion, soon to become the norm; and the
> institution of internal mechanisms of control, such as instilling the
> notion of submission as a woman's duty. The ground was thus pre-

pared, in other words, for the passing of a society in which women were active participants in the affairs of their community and for women's place in Arabian society to become circumscribed in the way that it already was for their sisters in the rest of the Mediterranean Middle East.

Marriage as sanctioned or practiced by Muhammad included polygamy and the marriage of girls nine and ten years old. Quranic utterances sanctioned the rights of males to have sexual relations with slave women (women bought or captured in war) and to divorce at will. In its fundamentals, the concept of marriage that now took shape was similar to that of Judaic marriage and similar, too, in some respects to Zoroastrian marriage, practiced by the ruling Iranian elite in the regions bordering Arabia. Not surprisingly, once the Islamic conquests brought about an intermingling of these socioreligious systems, Islam easily assimilated features of the others.[140]

El Saadawi sees this higher prestige enjoyed by women in Arab tribal societies symbolized in the importance given to some goddesses.[141] Three of these Meccan goddesses, Allat, Manat, and al 'Uzza, were acknowledged by Muhammad as "the daughters of Allah" when he sanctioned their worship during the period in Mecca when he was being persecuted. However, the verses sanctioning their worship were later abrogated by Muhammad, and Satan was held responsible for putting the verses on his tongue.[142] When Muhammad and his followers later conquered Mecca, he received the key to the Käa'bà from a woman, Sulafa. While Muslim sources downplay her importance, it should be noted that women of her tribe served as priestesses and soothsayers.[143]

Of prime importance to today's religious discourses is an understanding of the areas where Islam was founded and legally elaborated upon. These are identified by Ahmed as Arabia at the time when Islam was on the rise and Iraq in the period immediately following. In Arabia, Ahmed contends that Islam displaced a polytheistic religion where the three before-mentioned goddesses were paramount and where the patriarchal family unit was not the only option available. Muhammad was seen as a prophet in the Jewish and Christian traditions, and Islam adopted their monotheism with one god who was referred to by means of a male pronoun, as well as their customs of the patriarchal family and female subordination.[144] In the time after Muhammad's death and before the establishment of the Abbasid era (750-1258), Arabian women — including Muhammad's wives — enjoyed some prominence in areas such as warfare, religion, and marriage. However, they seem to have been a small elite and to have, in many instances, paid a high price for their tokenism. For example, the Khariji women warriors were killed and exposed naked by the "Orthodox," who opposed their participation in jihad (holy war).[145]

Islamic law, as codified in the Abbasid era, shows little cognizance of the quality and justice for women that is called for in Islam's ethical and spiritual context.[146] In fact, the Abbasid era may be characterized as an age which was particularly unfavorable to women. Even during this time, there were movements—those of the Sufis and the Qarmatians, for example—which questioned the laws.[147] Thus there existed the tensions between "Orthodox" Islam and the members of other Islamic sects. The former regarded Muhammad's practices and regulations, such as polygamy, nine-year-old child brides, the veiling of women, the confining of women, and the keeping of a concubine, as paramount; the latter regarded these practices as part of Muhammad's own social context and not binding on others in other contexts.[148]

As well as the women of Arabia, Ahmed contends that the women of ancient Egypt enjoyed a relatively egalitarian existence, as is evidenced by their "right to own, administer, and dispose of property, buy and sell, inherit and pass on property, testify in court, and act in all matters directly and without intermediary."[149] This is also testified to by an understanding which viewed marriage as a means for a shared life rather than for the production of heirs. (There is also little evidence for prostitution in the New Kingdom—1570-950 B.C.E.). If heirs were lacking, adoption was suggested as an option. However, while women enjoyed the prestigious role of priestess, and female goddesses such as Isis and Hathor were greatly honored, certain roles such as king, administrator, and scribe were generally closed to women. Ahmed contends that the role of women in Egypt successively declined during the Greek, the Roman, the Christian, and the Islamic eras.[150]

In our own times, and in the wider Islamic world, the low status of Muslim women is attested to by their literacy rate which, especially in rural areas, is among the lowest in the world. "Kept for centuries in physical, mental, and emotional confinement and deprived of the opportunity to actualize their human potential, most Muslim women find beyond their capability even the exercise of analyzing their personal life experiences as Muslim women."[151] However, in recent times, women with some amount of education and awareness are beginning to realize that what is called "islam-isation" is a cover for anti-women laws, grounded in a theology which is misogynistic and androcentric. Riffat Hassan contends that it is the myths, which shackle women, which must be changed. For example, Hassan speaks of the creation story and the creation of the human as female and male. She says that, in general, Muslims view the male as superior to the female and that this is based on three theological assumptions: first, that man is God's primary creation and woman, created from his rib, is secondary ontologically; second, that woman is primarily responsible for the Fall; third, that woman has an instrumental and not an essential existence—she is for man. Hassan sees the first issue as the most critical, for "if man and woman have been created equal by Allah, who is the ultimate arbiter of value, then they cannot become unequal, essentially, at a subsequent time. On the other hand, if man and woman have been created unequal by Allah, then they cannot become equal, essentially, at a subsequent time."[152] In the Qur'an itself there are no passages that suggest man was created prior to woman or that woman was derived from man; in fact, from a grammatical point of view, it could be argued that woman was created prior to man. It is in the *Hadith* (the sayings attributed to the prophet Muhammad) that the stories of woman being created from a rib arise. Hassan states that women must challenge these *ahadith* and demand a return to Qur'anic authenticity.[153] However, there is a further issue which Hassan does not address, that of both Allah and the human person being addressed in the Qur'an as male. Thus we read, for example:

Surah 75:Al-Qiyamah: "Then He [Allah] created and shaped and made of him [*sic*] two mates: the male and the female."

According to Fatima Mernissi, it is not so much that Muslim society is opposed to the equality of women as to the heterosexual unit. This is because this unit would get in the way of man's relationship to Allah by providing love, loyalty, and so on.[154] She contends that women are placed under male domination because they are feared as sexually powerful and that they are taught, in Muslim society, to be enemies.[155] In a later writing, Mernissa says that as a symbol of individualism, they are very much feared in the Arab world. In this world, men are slaves to Allah and masters to women; women are slaves to men, period.[156] However, rather than accepting the status quo, "Women are claiming power—corroding and ultimately destroying the foundation of Muslim hierarchy; whence the violence of the reaction and the rigidity of the response." She sees initiative as power.[157]

Islamic feminists today seem to be developing their own unique kind of feminism—a feminism which says that Islam, as it is practiced today, is patriarchal, but that it is not true Islam.[158] True Islam is to be found in the Qur'an—and, specifically, in the correct interpretation of the Qur'an. Thus, for example, while the Qur'an sanctions polygamy, saying it is legal to have as many as four wives, it also says all the wives must be treated equally. If a man thinks he cannot treat his wives equally, he is enjoined to have only one. But does the man judge this treatment for himself or is this an issue for the law to judge?[159] Passages such as "women are land which is yours to plough. ... You may therefore plough them whenever you wish," may prove more difficult to interpret from a woman's point of view.[160] At least one woman has suggested that the tension may reside with the Qur'an itself. Ahmed finds there two elements: the "pragmatic," which sanctions a hierarchical structure in marriage; and the "ethical," which is egalitarian in regard to the sexes. The problem lies in the fact that, throughout history, it is the pragmatists who have had control.[161] But this will change if women—and men—are willing to pay the price for the change. In fact, it *is* changing, both in the East and the West because there are women

who—breaking the bounds of femininity—become writers and think-
ers and take their stand against the reigning dogmas of the culture,
including a male dominance that trails in its wake emotional, psychological, and material brutality to women and children as religiously
sanctioned law and accepted social practice and demands that such
abuses be covered up in the name of loyalty to the culture.[162]

Our Mother, the Earth, and our Sister, the Divine Feminine, today suffer
this abuse with us. But so also will they rejoice with us in the time to come
if we together—men and women—are able to change our consciousness
and develop together a new world view that will truly honor and love the
whole of reality, including explicitly that which is feminine. This is our
necessary work if we are to survive through the twenty-first century. May
we prove capable of responding to this critical task which has been given
to the human at this time.

Epilogue

As the first streaks of light appeared in the sky, they appeared as black dots on the endless plain below. Training my binoculars on them, I found they were a herd of Black African Buffalo, fourteen in number. All were sleeping except for the one who stood as look-out in the center. Slowly, one by one, they stirred, rose to a standing position, and began to graze and move toward the East. It was idyllic.

But out of the corner of my eye — coming from the north — a lone buffalo was slowly approaching the herd. One member disengaged from the herd and went to meet the stranger. They communicated by assuming various positions in relationship to one another. The final message seemed to be, "It's all right; go ahead and meet the other members." The stranger was greeted by the other members one at a time. Sometimes they rubbed noses or merely acknowledged one another less intimately. The idyll continued.

Then, from the north, several other buffalo approached quickly and attempted to mingle rapidly with the herd. They were greeted with quick movements and the stomping of feet. They retreated speedily, only to return slowly, one by one, to be formally greeted and taken in by the herd.

Together, all moved off into the endless plain, grazing as they went. May it be so forever.

Notes

Introduction

1. Elizabeth Janeway, *Powers of the Weak* (New York: Alfred A. Knopf, 1980), 185.

2. Vandana Shiva, "Development, Ecology, and Women," in *Healing the Wounds: The Promise of Ecofeminism*, ed. Judith Plant (Philadelphia: New Society Publishers, 1989), 84. Italics are mine.

3. Ibid., 85.

4. Ibid., 84. However, in Shiva's view these "feminine" qualities have been expropriated from nature and women and transformed into qualities which belong exclusively to men.

5. See, for example, Sally B. Purvis, "Mothers, Neighbors and Strangers: Another Look at Agape," *Journal of Feminist Studies of Religion* 7, no. 1 (1991): 19-34. In this article, Purvis draws upon her own experience of motherhood as the basis for a contemporary model of agape seen from the perspective of a feminist ethic of care.

6. Merlin Stone, *When God Was a Woman* (New York: Dial Press, 1976), 22.

7. See Sallie McFague, *The Body of God: An Ecological Theology* (Minneapolis: Fortress Press, 1993) for a developed theology based on the metaphor of the Universe as the body of the Divinity.

8. I am indebted to a conversaton with Sydney Callahan for the understanding of the feminine and the masculine as a continuum.

9. Marilyn French, *Beyond Power: On Women, Men, and Morals* (New York: Summit Books, 1985), 442.

10. I view ecofeminism, in its broadest terms, as an understanding that there are well-defined parallels between the ways in which both women and the Earth are imaged and treated.

11. Ynestra King, "The Ecology of Feminism and the Feminism of Ecology" in *Healing the Wound*, ed. Plant, 18.

12. Marilyn Waring, *If Women Counted, A New Feminist Economics* (San Francisco: Harper & Row, 1988).

13. Maria Mies, *Women, The Last Colony* (London: Zed Books Ltd., 1988), 5.

14. Shiva, "Development, Ecology, and Women," 85.

15. Carolyn Merchant, *The Death of Nature: Ecology and the Scientific Revolution* (San Francisco: Harper & Row, 1983), xv-xvi.

16. Ibid., 2.

17. Rosemary Radford Ruether, *New Woman, New Earth* (New York: Seabury Press, 1975), 194-95.

18. The term *matricentric* appears to have been first used by Erich Fromm, *The*

Crisis of Psychoanalysis: Essays on Freud, Marx, and Social Psychology (New York: Holt, Rinehart and Winston, 1970), 104. For writings on the matricentric age, see, for example, Stone, *When God Was a Woman*; Marija Gimbutas, *The Goddesses and Gods of Old Europe, 6500-3500 B.C.* (Berkeley: University of California Press, 1982); Riane Eisler, *The Chalice and the Blade* (San Francisco: Harper & Row, 1987).

19. For a well-thought-out exposition of the construction of the present world-view, see Gerda Lerner, *The Creation of Patriarchy* (New York: Oxford University Press, 1986). One of the debated topics from prehistory is whether or not there actually was a time when warfare was not practiced. I found it noteworthy when, in 1990, a trip to Malaysia put me in contact with a group of indigenous people who have apparently never practiced warfare—even in response to others' violence.

20. Lynn White, Jr., "The Historical Roots of Our Ecologic Crisis," *Science* 155 (1967): 1207.

21. Ibid.

22. To cite an example, one could mention some members of the bioregional movement.

23. French, *Beyond Power*, 67-70.

24. Ibid., 304.

25. For an expanded statement on the matricentric and patriarchal ages, see Eleanor Rae and Bernice Marie-Daly, *Created in Her Image: Models of the Feminine Divine* (New York: Crossroad, 1990), 119-23.

26. Eli Sagan, *At the Dawn of Tyranny: The Origins of Individualism, Political Oppression, and the State* (New York: Alfred A. Knopf, 1985), 127-28.

27. Ibid., 134.

28. See Elizabeth A. Johnson, *She Who Is: The Mystery of God in Feminist Theological Discourse* (New York: Crossroad, 1992), for a comprehensive and well articulated theology of the Divinity as feminine Wisdom. However, this author would maintain that calling a work a feminist theology while still maintaining the use of the masculine word God is a basic contradiction. Further, the use of one divine attribute, Wisdom, as all-encompassing, is problematic.

1. The Present Situation of Women

1. DAWN, *Development Crisis and Alternative Visions: Third World Women's Perspectives* (Bergen: Christian Michelsen Institute, 1985), 21.

2. Mies, *Women: The Last Colony*, 159. The author of the particular chapter from which this information is taken is Veronika Bennholdt-Thomsen. It should be noted here that I am aware that neither do women account for all the poor nor are all women poor. Nor do I hold sexism to be the only "ism" that must be eliminated. One could mention, for example, racism, ageism, heterosexism, classism, nationalism, speciesism. However, I do hold sexism to be the primordial basis of all the isms and in this particular work, due to the nature of the subject matter, will focus primarily on this issue.

3. Marija Gimbutas, *The Language of the Goddess* (San Francisco: Harper & Row, 1989; London: Thames and Hudson, 1989), xiii, from the introduction by Joseph Campbell.

4. Ibid., xiii.

5. Ibid., xv. Gimbutas notes that only 2 to 3 percent of all the Old European figurines are male (175).

6. Ibid., xx-xxi. In summarizing the world-view of the culture of the Goddess, Gimbutas sees it as a celebration of life. She notes that, even at the death crisis, the first signs of regeneration appear. Further, even when they had the ability, there is no evidence of weapons and fortifications (321).

7. Murray Bookchin, *The Ecology of Freedom* (Palo Alto, CA: Cheshire Books, 1982), 57.

8. Eisler, *The Chalice and the Blade*, 53. Throughout, Eisler stresses that these ancient societies were not matriarchal but were based on a partnership rather than a dominator model.

9. Merlin Stone, *Ancient Mirrors of Womanhood, A Treasury of Goddess and Heroine Love from Around the World* (Boston: Beacon Press, 1979), 18.

10. Bookchin, *The Ecology of Freedom*, 63.

11. Peggy Reeves Sanday, *Female Power and Male Dominance: On the Origins of Sexual Inequality* (Cambridge: Cambridge University Press, 1981). This conclusion is drawn by Sanday as the result of the study of 150 tribal peoples. She also found that "there is a connection between religious thought and male and female power" (12).

12. Ibid. Rather than class as the basic element of the feminist-socialist critique of patriarchal capitalism, Iris Young, for example, also suggests that the key to the issue is the gender division of labor. See Iris Young, "Beyond the Unhappy Marriage: A Critique of the Dual Systems Theory," in *Women and Revolution: A Discussion of the Unhappy Marriage of Marxism and Feminism*, ed. Lydia Sargent (Boston: South End Press, 1981), 43-69. Eli Sagan, *At the Dawn of Tyranny*, also argues that tyranny against women (sexism) is found in the earliest societies while tyranny against certain men (classism) is not (248).

13. Mies, *Women: The Last Colony*, 69-70. For Mies, the asymmetric sexual division of labor can be attributed to the

predatory mode of production, or rather appropriation, which is based on the male monopoly over means of coercion, that is, arms, and on direct violence by means of which permanent relations of exploitation and dominance between the sexes were created and maintained.

The non-productive, *predatory mode of appropriation* became the paradigm of all exploitative relations between human beings. Its main mechanism is to transform autonomous human producers into conditions for production for others, or, to define them as "natural resources" for others (86).

But Mies's presentation of male dominance in terms of the use of weapons does not address the issue of why men choose to use weapons in the first place.

14. Sanday, *Female Power and Male Dominance*, 163-83.

15. Ibid., 163. Sanday is of the opinion that, if there is a basic difference of the sexes other than the biological difference, it rests in the fact that, as a group, women have been unwilling to risk death in violent conflict (210). Studies of the women who saw conflict in the armed services in the Gulf War may shed further light on her hypothesis.

16. Ibid.

17. French, *Beyond Power*, 260. French characterizes the power possessed by these women as personal rather than institutional. She sees an exception to this

rule—although a marginal one—in the monasteries of the eighth through twelfth centuries and some of the guilds of medieval Europe. French refers to this power as marginal because

> it was taken because male control was loose enough that no one specifically denied it to women or had the authority to enforce a denial. As soon as male control was centralized and solidified, men removed women from their positions and specifically excluded them from the institutions within which they had acted (260).

18. *Webster's New Universal Unabridged Dictionary* (New York: Dorset and Baber, 1979).

19. French, *Beyond Power*, 75.

20. Ibid., 94.

21. Ibid., 413.

22. Jürgen Moltmann, *God in Creation: A New Theology of Creation and the Spirit of God* (San Francisco: Harper & Row, 1985), 27.

23. George T. Montague, *The Holy Spirit: Growth of a Biblical Tradition* (New York: Paulist Press, 1976), 235.

24. Elizabeth Moltmann-Wendel, *A Land Flowing with Milk and Honey: Perspectives on Feminist Theology* (New York: Crossroad, 1982), 154.

25. Dorothy Dinnerstein, "Survival On Earth: The Meaning of Feminism" in *Healing the Wounds*, ed. Plant, 195. Dinnerstein posits two contrasting modes of power. The first she sees as hostile to life, damaging what it cannot succeed in actually killing or controlling. The other she calls nurturant power, a power which cherishes the freedom, health and integrity of what it loves. While she believes that they have coexisted in a fragile balance in the past, she now sees the balance as tipped to the death-wielding mode.

26. Janeway, *Powers of the Weak*, 108-22.

27. Ibid., 157-67.

28. Ibid., 165. An example from our recent past that we are still unwilling to face is our granting of total responsibility to George Bush to wage a war in the Gulf. It will be interesting to see if we do experience a sense of betrayal as a result.

29. French, *Beyond Power*, 76.

30. Janeway, *Powers of the Weak*, 168-85.

31. Ibid., 173.

32. Ibid., 179-80.

33. Eleanor H. Haney, *Vision and Struggle: Meditations on Feminist Spirituality and Politics* (Portland, ME: Astarte Shell Press, 1989), 109-14. Haney thinks that violence will be necessary in certain situations (114-18).

34. Janeway, *Powers of the Weak*, 181.

35. Ibid., 181.

36. See, for example, Yvonne Y. Haddad, *Women, Religion, and Social Change* (Albany: State University of New York Press, 1985), xii. This book is based on the thesis that "women take a more active part in public life, and in the establishment of new religious structures during periods of social crisis when the normal functioning of society breaks down." With this understanding, Women-Church is a to-be-expected sign of the times.

37. Haney, *Vision and Struggle*, 88.

38. Moltmann, *God in Creation*, 195.

39. French, *Beyond Power*, 499-500.

40. Haney, *Vision and Struggle*, 61-65.

41. Elise Boulding, *The Underside of History: A View of Women Through Time* (Boulder, CO: Westview Press, 1976), 531.

42. See, for example, Donald W. Dayton, "Pneumatological Issues in the Holiness Movement," in *Spirit of Truth: Ecumenical Perspectives on the Holy Spirit*, ed. Theodore Stylianopoulos and S. Mark Heim (Brookline, MA: Holy Cross Orthodox Press, 1986), 156. Dayton sees feminism as the natural extension of the anti-slave hermeneutic to women, based on Galatians 3:28.

43. As quoted by Angela Y. Davis, *Women, Race and Class* (New York: Vintage Books, 1983), 83. Davis notes that by 1869 Sojourner Truth had decided to go with expediency—men first—rather than principle—all adults. It is not clear to me what brought about this change in her thinking.

44. Jo Freeman, "Women and Public Policy: An Overview," in *Women, Power and Policy*, ed. Ellen Boneparth (New York: Pergamon Press, 1982), 52.

45. Ibid., 52-53.

46. bell hooks, *Feminist Theory: From Margin to Center* (Boston: South End Press, 1984). Also see Davis, *Women, Race and Class*, for a reading by a black activist on the women's movement as a conflict between the white middle class and the working class/people of color. While Davis's work is helpful in providing a context for perceiving the women's movement, she seems to succumb to the error that people in the movement are not free and capable of setting their own goals. Rather, the goals seem to be dictated by those outside the movement.

47. These two examples are personal observations based, in the former case, on a recent visit to Asia and, in the latter instance, on informal input given by the representatives of nongovernmental organizations in Geneva at the U.N. in August of 1991 at the preparatory conference for the United Nations Conference on Environment and Development.

48. Gloria Joseph, "The Incompatible Menage a Trois: Marxism, Feminism, and Racism," in *Women and Revolution*, ed. Lydia Sargent (Boston: South End Press, 1981), 95. Joseph offers the further claim that the insight that the "personal is political" was long the insight of the blacks and was picked up by the feminists. She says applying this insight to blacks would necessitate the inclusion of males, an inclusion which she sees as "extremely problematic for radical feminists" (97).

49. Sometimes these issues can contain a certain amount of humor. I shall share one personal experience as an example. Upon being appointed to a prestigious dioceasan commitee, my employer said that, since the other chair was very well situated—including membership in the DAR—I was not to make mention of my own parental background; and if I did not, no one would ever guess!

50. Leila Ahmed, "Feminism and Feminist Movements in the Middle East, A Preliminary Exploration: Turkey Egypt, Algeria, People's Democratic Republic of Yemen," in *Women and Islam*, ed. Azizah al-Hibri (Oxford: Pergamon Press, 1982), 161-63. However, Ahmed cites the women of the Arabian peninsula as not subject to these conflicts because they do their own social analysis out of an indigenous tradition (167-68). She also cites Fatima Mernissi as an exception to the rule of conflict within oneself (163).

51. Nawal el Saadawi, "Women and Islam," in *Women and Islam*, ed. al-Hibri,

193. This submission is made explicit by passages from the Qur'an such as "Women are land which is yours to plough. . . . You may therefore plough them whenever you wish (201).

52. Fatima Mernissi, *Beyond the Veil: Male-Female Dynamics in a Modern Muslim Society* (Cambridge, MA: Schenkman Publishing, 1975), xvi.

53. Ibid., viii.

54. Ibid., xvi-xvii.

55. Valerie Saiving Goldstein, "The Human Situation: A Feminine Viewpoint," in *The Nature of Man: In Theological and Psychological Perspective*, ed. Simon Doniger (New York: Harper and Brothers, 1962), 151.

56. Ibid., 165.

57. This statement was validated by my own work with women in the diocese of Bridgeport, Connecticut. In listening to women in hearings for the "Bishops' Pastoral on Women," the one recurring theme was lack of self-esteem. Differences in socioeconomic background did not appear to be a factor in this perception of self.

58. Rae and Marie-Daly, *Created in Her Image*.

59. Katherine K. Young, "Introduction," in *Women in World Religions*, ed. Arvind Shama (Albany: State University of New York Press, 1987), 28.

60. Donna Marie Wulff, "Images and Roles of Women in Bengali Vaisnava padāvalī kīrtan" in *Women, Religion, and Social Change*, ed. Haddad, 217-45.

61. Korean Association of Women Theologians, "Feminist Theological Lighting on Goddess Image Imposed on Korean Folk Beliefs," *In God's Image* (September 1990), 51.

62. El Saadawi, "Women and Islam," 194.

63. See, for example, Margaret A. Farley, "A New Form of Communion: Feminism and the Chinese Church," in *In God's Image* 10, no. 3 (1991), 51.

64. Shiva, "Development, Ecology, and Women," 87. It should be noted that the environmental crisis is not only a product of recent Western culture. For example, the deforestation of India had been effected by A.D. 800 and of China by A.D. 1000. The soils of the Middle East were ruined even earlier, as were those of southern Italy and Sicily. See, for example, Gary Snyder, *Turtle Island* (New York: New Directions, 1974), 106-7. What may be significant is the rate at which this destruction is now occurring and the fact that it is worldwide. For example, satellite pictures of the Earth show large portions of South America and Africa in flames.

65. Vandana Shiva, *Staying Alive: Women, Ecology and Development* (London: Zed, 1988), 10-11. Shiva notes that the key to producing real poverty may be human technologies as, for example, in Ethiopia.

66. Shiva, *Staying Alive*, 41-42.

67. Ibid., 46. Gimbutas, *The Language of the Goddess*, also notes this linking of women and nature in the prehistoric understanding of the Earth as mother which survives in the agricultural communities of Europe to the present day. She notes that in all European languages, the Earth is feminine (141).

68. Ibid. Shiva devotes a whole chapter to women as silviculturalists (55-95); to women as agriculturalists (96-179); and to women as managers of water resources (181-217).

69. Ibid., 64.

70. Ibid., 67-95.

71. Ibid., 96.

72. Ibid.

73. Ibid.

74. Ibid., 183.

75. Ibid., 211-12.

76. French, *Beyond Power*, 304. The first principle is false because men are as much bound by nature as are women, plants, birds, and so forth.

77. Ibid., 297-98.

78. Bookchin, *The Ecology of Freedom*, 251.

79. Lerner, *The Creation of Patriarchy*, 217.

80. Penina V. Adelman, "New Rituals, Ancient Traditions," *Woman of Power* 19 (1991): 30. Specifically, Adelman has used Rosh Hodesh, the monthly holiday marking the new moon, as the means for women to apprehend the Shekhina, the Divine Presence in this world.

81. Diana Y. Paul *Women in Buddhism: Images of the Feminine in Mahāyāna Tradition* (Berkeley: University of California Press, 1985), ix.

82. Diana L. Eck and Devaki Jain, ed., *Speaking of Faith: Global Perspectives on Women, Religion and Social Change* (Philadelphia: New Society Publishers, 1987), 73-74. The editors go on to say that demythologizing our images is not the answer because images cannot be replaced by facts; they can only be replaced by other images (74). It will be worth noting how the reunification of the two Germanies affects the legal status of women in the long term. The announcement of the reunification was not received as a blessing by at least some East German women, who perceived it as the avenue by which their status and rights would be lessened.

83. Devaki Jain, "Gandhian Contribution Toward a Feminist Ethis," in *Speaking of Faith*, ed. Eck and Jain, 277. As well as seeing the need to identify this common universal core, Jain also notes the need to "mark out the boundary areas which may be different" (277).

84. Ibid., 286-88.

85. Fatima Mernissi, "Femininity as Subversion: Reflections on the Muslim Concept of Nūshuz," in *Speaking of Faith*, ed. Eck and Jain, 95-108.

86. Mies, *Women: The Last Colony*, 154-55. Mies reaches several conclusions on women's emancipation process as a result of this experience. They include the following:

(1) That the sexism struggle and the class struggle cannot be separated.

(2) That it is wrong for women to suppress their struggle against male oppression in the name of class unity.

(3) That people from outside are not needed as consciousness-raisers but as initiators and coordinators.

(4) That collective leadership can be effective.

(5) That an appropriate physical setting is necessary in order to provide democratic participation.

(6) That separate and autonomous women's organizations based on class can strengthen rather than weaken the class (155-56).

It would seem that there are many elements in the model which could be applied to the "developed" countries as well.

2. Ecofeminism

1. Val Plumwood, "Ecofeminism: An Overview and Discussion of Positions and Arguments," in *Women and Philosophy*, ed. Jana L. Thompson (*Australian Journal of Philosophy*, supplement to vol. 64, 1986), 120.

2. Ibid., 120. For an initial primer in the area of ecofeminism that incorporates vast scholarship as well as depth of feeling, see Susan Griffin, *Woman and Nature: The Roaring Inside Her* (New York: Harper Colophen Books, 1978).

3. Carolyn Merchant, "Ecofeminism and Feminist Theory," in *Reweaving the World: The Emergence of Ecofeminism*, ed. Irene Diamond and Gloria Orenstein (San Francisco: Sierra Club Books, 1990), 100. Cf., Francoise d'Eaubonne, "Feminism or Death," in *New French Feminisms: An Anthology*, ed. Elain Marks and Isabelle de Courtivron (Amherst: University of Massachusetts, 1980).

4. Charlene Spretnak, "Ecofeminism: Our Roots and Flowering," in *Reweaving the World*, ed. Diamond and Orenstein. Spretnak further notes: "Ecofeminism grew out of radical, or cultural, feminism (rather than from liberal feminism or socialist feminism), which holds that identifying the dynamics—largely fear and resentment—behind the dominance of male over female is the key to comprehending every expression of patriarchal culture with its hierarchical, militaristic, mechanistic, industrialist forms" (5).

5. Introduction, *Reweaving the World*, ed. Diamond and Orenstein, x. The editors make the point that women's bodies are wonderful indicators of the health—or sickness—of our planet.

6. Carolyn Merchant, "Feminism and Ecology," in *Deep Ecology: Living as if Nature Mattered*, ed., Bill Devall and George Sessions (Layton, UT: Gibbs M. Smith, 1985), 229-31.

7. Karen J. Warren, "Feminism and Ecology: Making Connections," *Environmental Ethics* 9, no. 1 (1987): 3-20.

8. King, "The Ecology of Feminism," 19-20.

9. Karen J. Warren and Jim Cheney, "Ecological Feminism and Ecosystem Ecology," *Hypatia* 6, no. 1 (1991): 180-81.

10. Lee Quinby, "Ecofeminism and the Politics of Resistance," in *Reweaving the World*, ed. Diamond and Orenstein, 124.

11. Ibid., 124. Quinby contrasts this to theory in the perscriptive mode—the "creed."

12. Ibid., 126-27. Quinby's understanding of the value of ecofeminism parallels that of Starhawk, who sees that "the contribution of feminism to ecology is its critique of power relations." Cf. Starhawk, "Feminist Earth-based Spirituality and Ecofeminism," in *Healing the Wounds*, ed. Plant, 181.

13. French, *Beyond Power*, 445. While French is referring here to feminism rather than ecofeminism, given her whole thrust, it appears that the extension of her thinking into ecofeminism is warranted. For French, "the entire thrust of feminism is to create a revolution worth living for" (457).

14. Ibid., 18.

15. Ibid., 104. French goes on to note: "The nature-culture dichotomy is probably most prominent in societies in which control is seen as a high good" (109).

16. Margot Adler, "Eco-Feminism: A Women's History Month Special," WBAI (March 27, 1990).

17. Shiva, *Staying Alive*, 3. Shiva goes on to note:

Fragmentation and uniformity as assumed categories of progress and development destroy the living forces which arise from relationships within the "web of life" and the diversity in the elements and patterns of these relationships (3).

18. Sherry B. Ortner, "Is Female to Male as Nature Is to Culture?" in *Woman, Culture and Society*, ed. Michele Zimbalist Rosaldo and Louis Lamphere (Stanford, CA: Stanford University Press, 1974).

19. Spretnak, "Ecofeminism," 8. See Spretnak for specific conferences and books engendered by this issue.

20. King, "The Ecology of Feminism," 22-23. I am not sure that two and three should be considered different models; rather, they are the same response taking different paths to create a new culture. King herself might agree with this comment as, in a later article, she classifies those who have repudiated the women/nature connection as radical rationalist feminists, while she calls those who value and celebrate both women and nature radical cultural feminists. See Ynestra King, "Healing the Wounds: Feminism, Ecology, and the Nature/Culture Dualism," in *Reweaving the World*, ed. Diamond and Orenstein, 110-13.

21. French, *Beyond Power*, 71. French's questioning of the validity of the analogy is reinforced by a group of studies by anthropologists, many making use of populations in New Guinea, Africa, and South America, which present evidence that Ortner's nature:culture::women:men equation is not a valid one with these populations. See Carol B. MacCormack and Marilyn Strathern, eds., *Nature, Culture and Gender* (Cambridge: Cambridge University Press, 1980).

22. Catherine Roach, "Loving Your Mother: On the Woman-Nature Relation," *Hypatia* 6, no. 1 (1991): 53-54.

23. Shiva, *Staying Alive*, 4-5.

24. Judith Plant, "Searching for Common Ground: Ecofeminism and Bioregionalism," in *Reweaving the World*, ed. Diamond and Orenstein, 156.

25. Beverly W. Harrison. "A Theology of Pro-Choice: A Feminist Perspective on Abortion," in *Speaking of Faith*, ed. Eck and Jain, 218. Worthy of note on this issue is French's observation:

> Almost always sexual freedom in women is blamed for a general moral "depravity" and held responsible for the demise of a class or state. The connection is unclear, but perhaps it lies in a sense that women would not have sexual freedom if men had not abandoned tight control over them, and that men's abandonment of control leads to "decadence" (*Beyond Power*, 95).

26. Patricia Jagentowicz Mills, "Feminism and Ecology: On the Domination of Nature," *Hypatia* 6, no. 1 (1991): 167. I agree with Mill's perception that nature is not all good, as evidenced by natural disasters such as earthquakes, volcanic eruption, and so forth.

27. Ruether, *New Woman, New Earth*, 196-97.

28. Joanna Macy, "Awakening to the Ecological Self," in *Healing the Wounds*, ed. Plant, 209.

29. Ibid., 210.

30. Ariel Kay Salleh, "Deeper than Deep Ecology, the Eco-feminist Connection," *Environmental Ethics* 6 (1984): 339-45. However, it should be noted that Salleh thinks that men can change if they learn to love the woman inside themselves.

31. Michael E. Zimmerman, "Deep Ecology and Ecofeminism: The Emerging Dialogue," in *Reweaving the World*, ed. Diamond and Orenstein, 138-41.

32. Ibid., 141-42.

33. Ibid., 142.

34. Val Plumwood, "Nature, Self, and Gender: Feminism, Environmental Philosophy, and the Critique of Rationalism," *Hypatia* 6, no. 1 (1991): 20.

35. Plumwood, "Ecofeminism," 120.

36. Plumwood, "Nature, Self and Gender," 18-19. For Plumwood, "the inferiorization of both women and nature is grounded in rationalism, and the connections of both to the inferiorizing of the body, hierarchical concepts of labor and disembedded and individualist accounts of the self" (22). It is this same rationalism or oppositionally construed reason that is the key to anthropomorphism; this being the case, one cannot look for the solution to today's problems, problems created by this thinking, in a rationalist dualism such as the neo-Kantism espoused by some deep ecologists (6).

37. Elizabeth Dodson Gray, *Green Paradise Lost* (Wellesley, MA: Roundtable Press, 1981), 5-6. Gray notes:

[Lynn White, Jr.] correctly perceived that the pagan animistic view (which affirmed the presence of "spirit" in the lower realms of trees and rocks and streams) functioned to protect nature in a way that the pyramidal paradigm of the Judeo-Christian biblical world-view (which locates "spirit" only in the human and above) does not (5).

38. Ruether, *New Woman, New Earth*, 194.

39. H. Patricia Hynes, *The Recurring Silent Spring* (New York: Pergamon Press, 1989). Hynes identifies herself as a feminist and a former employee of the Environmental Protection Agency.

40. Carol J. Adams, "Ecofeminism and the Eating of Animals," *Hypatia* 6, no. 1 (1991): 137-40. Adams questions why we romanticize the Native American peoples who hunted animals instead of honoring those Native Americans who were horticulturalists and primarily vegetarians (139).

41. Ibid., 140. See also, Marti Kheel, "Ecofeminism and Deep Ecology: Reflections on Identity and Difference," in *Reweaving the World*, ed. Diamond and Orenstein, 136-37. Kheel talks about the male's need to differentiate by separating from mother and from nature—from nature by killing animals with which he somehow identifies. Kheel sees men as using women and animals for their psychological needs (instrumentalism).

42. Plumwood, "Nature, Self, and Gender," 21.

43. *The Dictionary of Philosophy*, ed. Dagobert D. Runes (New York: Philosophical Library, 1942), 84. Examples cited include Platonic dualism (the sensible and the intelligible worlds); Cartesian dualism (thinking and extended substances); Leibnizian dualism (possible and actual worlds); Kantian dualism (phenomenal and noumenal worlds). When the term first appeared in 1700, it was in relationship to the religious terms of *good* and *evil*.

44. See Stephanie Leland, "Feminism and Ecology: Theoretical Connections," in *Reclaim the Earth: Women Speak Out for Life on Earth*, ed. Leonie Caldecott and Stephanie Leland (London: The Women's Press, 1983), 67-72, for an understanding of dualism as a necessary stage in evolution. The author now sees us as suffering from a great imbalance of masculinism and as needing to reclaim the feminine principle to save the Earth and all its inhabitants.

45. Grace M. Jantzen, "Healing our Brokenness: The Spirit and Creation," *The Ecumenical Review* 42, no. 2 (1990): 131.

46. Ibid., 133.

47. Ibid., 132. However, the body is not "an inert innocent lump" but has "a kind of negative power of its own, especially strong and sinister in the case of sexuality" (132).

48. Ibid., 137. In regard to the meaning of the "other," Ynestra King makes the interesting observation that "objectification is forgetting." See Ynestra King, "Feminism and the Revolt of Nature," *Heresies* 4, no. 1 (1981): 15.

49. Grace M. Jantzen, *God's World, God's Body* (Philadelphia: The Westminster Press, 1984), 148.

50. Catherine Keller, "Women Against Wasting the World: Notes on Eschatology and Ecology," in *Reweaving the World*, ed. Diamond and Orenstein, 255. This stance becomes even more terrifying if, in fact, Keller is correct in her understanding that it is backed by "the full secular force of U.S. industrial-imperial power" (255).

51. Rosemary Ruether, "Christianity," in *Women in World Religions*, ed. Sharma, 228-29. Ruether sees this new understanding of a theology of creation as being the basis of all liberation theologies, including the feminist.

52. Ibid., 208.

53. Ibid.

54. See., e.g., Elizabeth Schüssler-Fiorenza, *In Memory of Her: A Feminist Theological Reconstruction of Christian Origins* (New York: Crossroad, 1985).

55. Ruether, *New Woman, New Earth*, 196.

56. "The 1992 World Development Report on Environment and Development," in *UNCED Network News*, no. 3, published by the World Bank (1991): 13-14.

57. French, *Beyond Power*, 534.

58. Ruether, *New Woman, New Earth*, 198-201. Ruether cites Reinhold Neibuhr as the "chief formulator of this essential dichotomy in bourgeois culture between the home and public life" (199).

59. Barbara E. Reed, "Taoism," in *Women in World Religions*, ed. Sharma, 165-66.

60. Charlene Spretnak, *The Politics of Women's Spirituality* (Garden City, New York: Anchor Books, 1982), states that yin does not represent passivity exclusively but rather has been composed to wu wei "non-action." Wu wei has been taken to mean "refraining from actions against nature, thus acting in harmony with the Tao." It denotes a consciousness of oneness (xxix).

61. James Gleick, *Chaos: Making a New Science* (New York: Viking Penguin, 1987), 309.

62. Ruether, "Christianity," 207-10. Ruether sees this minority view of female/male as the dominant view in today's liberal churches (209).

63. Carol Ochs, *Behind the Sex of God: Toward a New Consciousness—Transcending Matriarchy and Patriarchy* (Boston: Beacon Press, 1977), 139.

64. Jantzen, *God's World, God's Body*, 122-30.

65. Young, "Introduction," in *Women in World Religions*, ed. Sharma, 9. I am drawn here to reflect on the similarities to the idea of "separate but equal," impossible to realize within a society which was (is) racist.

66. Hazel Henderson, "The Warp and the Weft: The Coming Synthesis of Eco-Philosophy and Eco-Feminism," in *Reclaim the Earth*, ed. Caldecott and Leland, 209-10.

67. Thomas Berry, *The Dream of the Earth*, (San Francisco: Sierra Club Books, 1988), 138-39.

68. Merchant, *The Death of Nature*, 42-43.

69. David Tracy, "The Influence of Feminist Theory on My Theological Work," *Journal of Feminist Studies in Religion* 7, no. 1 (1991): 122-23.

70. Ibid., 123.

71. Ibid.

72. Diana L. Eck, *Darśan: Seeing the Divine Image in India* (Chambersburg, PA: Anima Books, 1985), 24. One wonders if this ability to embrace both unity and diversity is in part explained by Hinduism's emphasis on the image rather than the word (20). (This is not to deny a very rich literary corpus which is also a part of Hinduism.)

73. I see this as an implication in the Lukan gospel, Chapter 7, verse 35.

74. Jantzen, *God's World, God's Body*, 149.

75. Ibid., 152. Is this not in fact what a human parent, friend, lover, also does?

76. Ibid., 157-58.

77. Plumwood, "Nature, Self, and Gender," 19.

78. Ibid., 20. Jantzen finds the source of separation in white males residing in the alienation of the bodily dimension. She argues that this alienation results in fear and projection onto those who are defined as feeling and sexual, that is, those associated with the body. She believes that this issue must be dealt with on the practical rather than the theoretical level, for example, by embracing the other as Francis did the leper. Jantzen, "Healing Our Brokenness," 139-41.

79. Ibid., 20.

80. Ibid., 13.

81. Rosemary Radford Ruether, "Toward an Ecological-Feminist Theology of Nature," in *Healing the Wounds*, ed. Plant, 145-50.

3. Living the Earth-Centered Future Today

1. Since there is no form on Earth—whether river or mountain, wild flower or elephant seal—which is not alive with energy, for the purposes of my writing I have chosen simply to designate all as life forms.

2. Lester R. Brown, "Launching the Environmental Revolution," in *State of the World* (New York: W. W. Norton & Company, 1992), 190.

3. Berry, *The Dream of the Earth*, 120. See Berry and Brian Swimme, *The Universe Story* (San Francisco: HarperCollins, 1992), for a telling of this single story from the primordial flaring forth to the present and into the next millenium.

4. Ibid., 128-32. If, in fact, it is true that "values are more compelling if they are invested with divine authority and continually symbolized in rites that appeal to the senses," as is claimed by Clyde Kluckhorn in the Foreword to *Reader in Comparative Religion*, ed. William A. Lessa and Evon Z. Vogt (Evanston, IL: Row, Peterson and Company, 1958), v, then the part religion can play in developing values is indeed a critical one.

5. Heidi Hartmann, "The Unhappy Marriage of Marxism and Feminism: Towards a More Progressive Union," in *Women and Revolution: A Discussion of the Unhappy Marriage of Marxism and Feminism*, ed. Lydia Sargent (Boston: South End Press, 1981), 10. I often reflect back on my travels through Poland, Czechoslovakia, Hungary, Yugoslavia, and East Germany shortly before the collapse of the Soviet

empire. Those we met saw the sharpest contrast between East and West to be in the fact that the peoples in the East had their basic needs, such as food, housing, medical care, education, and child care as rights which were provided, while we in the West did not. It seems that, while their means for meeting these needs was inappropriate, the goal was humane; in the West, neither our means nor our ends are humane.

6. While written many years prior to the Gulf War, French, *Beyond Power*, 260, offers this prescient comment: "Non-Western societies have not gone so far in 'masculinizing' culture as the West, and therefore do not present as great a threat to the continuation of life on the planet. The West is the most important area of concentration in a study of a morality of power because it has carried that morality to the greatest extreme." This morality of power, because we have the weapons to do so, has put us in the position of being the world's ultimate terrorist state. Of course, there is no reason to doubt that the non-Western states will not behave likewise if (or when) they have the means to do so.

7. Elizabeth Dodson Gray, *Patriarchy as a Conceptual Trap* (Wellesley, MA: Roundtable Press, 1982), 76-77. Concretely, Dodson Gray asks why we never hear about Eleanor Roosevelt and the United Nations Declaration on Human Rights — a positive accomplishment — but rather about the Marshall Plan and the Truman Doctrine and Yalta.

8. Gary Snyder, *Turtle Island* (New York: New Directions, 1974), 108-9.

9. See, John Seed, Joanna Macy, Pat Fleming, Arne Naess, *Thinking Like a Mountain: Towards a Council of All Beings* (Philadelphia: New Society Publishers, 1988) for a short but comprehensive guidebook on experiencing a Council of All Beings. This author first attempted this experience, with much trepidation, in a group totally unrelated to environmental issues and found that all were able to be in touch with other life forms and relate back to the group in ways that were truly moving.

10. Think how much richer our meetings would be if all were part of our decision-making processes:

A. aspen, algae, alligators, agate, Adirondacks, etc.

B. beetles, boa constrictors, birch, Black Sea, beavers, etc.

C. crocus, cows, Connecticut River Valley, canaries, crustaceans, etc.

11. Patrick D. Murphy, "Ground, Pivot, Motion: Ecofeminist Theory, Dialogics, and Literary Practice," in *Hypatia* 6, no. 1 (1991): 151.

12. Bookchin, *The Ecology of Freedom*, 364-65. We may also need to look at these values in new ways. Thus, for example, Raimundo Panikkar suggests that freedom is not the capacity to choose but its opposite — spontaneity. He describes it as being the source of creativity that is deep within the self; as present in acts which are not conditioned by need; as the unique event. Raimundo Panikkar, "Chosen and Universal: Affirming a Christian Radical Pluralism," lecture, Kirkridge Retreat Center, Bangor, PA, October 5-7, 1990.

13. "The Challenge of Environmental Sustainability," booklet, Merrickville, Ontario, Canada: Guideposts for a Sustainable Future: 1. The author(s) sees sustainability as a realizable goal if we can reach social consensus on the need for sustainability and if we reach this consensus in time for the Earth to rebuild the ecosystems (3).

14. Ibid., 2.

15. Charlene Spretnak, *The Spiritual Dimension of Green Politics* (Santa Fe, NM: Bear & Company, 1986), 22-23.

16. Peter Berg, "Growing a Life-Place Politics," in *Home! A Bioregional Reader*, ed. Van Andruss, Christopher Plant, Judith Plant, and Eleanor Wright (Philadelphia: New Society Publishers, 1990), 137-43. Berg sees the neighborhoods (what he calls "socialsheds" of neighbors) joining together to form watershed councils which, in time, would join other watershed councils to form bioregional congresses, such as the May 1992 Turtle Island Bioregional Congress V. He also sees the need, if the goals of sustainability are to be met, for alliances with Native American groups, deep ecologists, and Earth-spirit women's groups (143).

17. Francis Moore Lappé, *Diet for a Small Planet* (New York: Ballantine Books, 1991).

18. Jim Dodge, "Living by Life: Some Bioregional Theory and Practice," in *Home!* ed. Andruss, et al., 12. Dodge, relying on Marshall Sahlins, notes that there are two ways to affluence: though increased production, or through reduced needs. We who are theologians might well put our minds to developing a much needed "theology of enoughness."

19. Snyder, *Turtle Island*, 97.

20. Fritjof Capra and Charlene Spretnak, *Green Politics* (New York: E. P. Dutton, 1984), 195. Capra and Spretnak are here referring to a study conducted by the research institute SRI International.

21. Rosemary Radford Ruether, *Sexism and God-Talk: Toward a Feminist Theology* (Boston: Beacon Press, 1983), 72-92. I am reminded of the remark made by Judith Moyers at the United Nations preview of the "Spirit and Nature" film (June 5, 1991), that, if the human were no longer on the planet, the only ones to miss us would be our pets, and they only for a short time.

22. Judith Plant, "The Circle Is Gathering," in *Healing the Wounds*, ed. Plant, 251. It may well be that Plant's use of the word *compassion* — to suffer with — will provide a better basis for the developing ecofeminist ethics than the word *care*.

23. Karen J. Warren, "The Power and the Promise of Ecological Feminism," *Environmental Ethics* 12:2 (1990): 144.

24. Ibid., 144.

25. Ibid.

26. Ibid.

27. Ibid., 125.

28. Ibid., 131.

29. Carol P. Christ, "Rethinking Theology and Nature," in *Reweaving the World*, ed. Diamond and Orenstein, 66.

30. Diamond and Orenstein, *Reweaving the World*, xi-xii.

31. Shiva, "Development, Ecology, and Women," 84. This would also be the concern with the program that is being developed by the National Council of Catholic Women. If the Earth is only looked upon as resource, this would appear to be just an extension of the consciousness that created the problem rather than an articulation of the new consciousness needed to heal the Earth.

32. Snyder, *Turtle Island*, 103.

33. Thomas Berry, "Dawn Over the Earth: The Emerging Ecozoic Era," Earth Ethics Forum '91, St. Leo College, North Tampa, FL, May 10-12, 1991.

34. Deane Curtin, "Toward an Ecological Ethic of Care," *Hypatia* 6, no. 1 (1991): 65-67.

35. Kheel, "Ecofeminism and Deep Ecology," 136-37. Kheel comes to this emphasis on the particular in the context of questioning the whole — the expanded self — as abstract and as involving the killing of the other.

36. Boulding, *The Underside of History*, 326.

37. Curtin, "Toward an Ecological Ethic of Care," 67-68.

38. Murphy, "Ground, Pivot, Motion," 147.

39. Ibid., 151.

40. Ibid.

41. Ibid., 152. Murphy cites as non-valid renderings of the Earth's voices those based on instrumental reason such as Ronald Reagan's remark about trees as polluters and James Lovelock's assertion that Gaia will take care of herself, unless we have decided that she is determined to "commit biospheric suicide" (152-53).

42. Ibid.

43. Roger J.H. King, "Caring About Nature: Feminist Ethics and the Environment," *Hypatia* 6, no. 1 (1991): 84-85.

44. Jim Cheney, "Postmodern Environmental Ethics: Ethics as Bioregional Narrative," *Environmental Ethics* 11 (1989): 126-32. Cheney sees that "bioregionalism is a natural extension of the line of thought being developed by those advocating a view of ethics as contextualist and narrative" (128).

45. King, "Caring about Nature," 85.

46. Ibid., 87.

47. French, *Beyond Power*.

48. Sagan, *At the Dawn of Tyranny*.

49. Paul Shannon, "Peacework" (Cambridge, MA: The American Friends Service Committee, June, 1991).

50. Berry, *The Dream of the Earth*, 38. He goes on to say: "Until we have explained this situation to ourselves, we will never break the spell that has seized us. We will continue to be subject to this fatal attraction."

51. Ibid., 19.

52. Julia Scofield Russell, "The Evolution of an Ecofeminist," in *Reweaving the World*, ed. Diamond and Orenstein, 229. At our first C:WED Conference, held on January 18, 1992, in Norwalk, Connecticut, the five presenters shared how we had each "entered the Web" and elicited from the participants their entry point. It was very powerful.

53. Bookchin, *The Ecology of Freedom*, 316-17.

54. Berry, *The Dream of the Earth*, 194.

55. Ibid., 195. Berry gives as an example of our genetic coding the power of speech, whereas the cultural coding would be the form that speech takes. (200). One is lead to speculate whether Earthlings, in some distant future, might be genetically coded so that war would no longer be perceived as a possible response option to conflict.

56. Ibid., 194. Berry goes on to note that, in the West, we have deliberately set our cultural coding in opposition to our genetic coding (202). By so doing, we have turned ourselves into a dreamless people (203).

57. Ibid., 195.

58. Ibid., 58.

59. Starhawk, "Power, Authority, and Mystery: Ecofeminism and Earth-Based Spirituality," in *Reweaving the World*, ed. Diamond and Orenstein, 80-81. See the illustration on page 81. In this illustration, the branches symbolize the future.

60. Ibid., 82.

61. Ibid., 82-83.

62. Ibid., 83-85.

63. French, *Beyond Power*, 330.

64. Ibid., 334.

65. Haney, *Vision and Struggle*, 74-76.

66. Susan Griffin, "Curves Along the Road," in *Reweaving the World*, ed. Diamond and Orenstein, 88. Griffin contends that it is our ability to see in fragments — to deny reality — to make someone "other," that enables us to commit the horrors of nuclear holocaust, the concentration camps of the Nazis, mass starvation today, and prostitution (87-99).

67. Berry, *The Dream of the Earth*, 178. Berry speaks here of our need to make covenants with rivers and land and regions. He also speaks of the covenant made between the Divinity and the Earth and every creature of flesh, the sign of which was the rainbow. I cannot help but contrast the Divine rainbow sign with the human sign dedicated at the United Nations Conference on Environment and Development (Brazil 1992) — that of a needle piercing the sky.

68. Judith Plant, "Searching for Common Ground: Ecofeminism and Bioregionalism," in *Reweaving the World*, ed. Diamond and Orenstein, 158-59. Plant sees both as sharing an understanding of the importance of process — the *how* being as critical as the *what* (159).

69. Cheney, "Postmodern Environmental Ethics," 128.

70. Marnie Muller, "Bioregionalism/Western Culture/Women," in *Home!*, ed. Andruss, et al., 87-88.

71. Plumwood, "Nature, Self, and Gender," 20-21.

72. Shiva, *Staying Alive*, 10-11. The value of the lifestyles of these women and tribal peoples is not usually recognized. This may be because, as Shiva says: "The more effectively the cycles of life, as essential ecological processes, are maintained, the more invisible they become. Disruption is violent and visible; balance and harmony are experienced, not seen" (44).

73. Berry, *The Dream of the Earth*, 166. Mapping is an important priority in the bioregional movement. See, for example, Doug Abernathy, *Bioregional Primer: A Mapping Guide* (Edinburgh, Scotland: Edinburgh School of Environmental Design, 1992).

74. Ibid., 166-68.

75. Ibid., 163. Berry notes: "If there is to be any true progress, then the entire life community must progress. Any progress of the human at the expense of the larger life community must ultimately lead to a diminishment of human life itself. A degraded habitat will produce degraded humans. An enhanced habitat supports an elevated mode of the human" (165).

76. Ibid., 166-68.

77. Ibid., 167. Berry contends that the instruction given us through the natural world is the only way for the human species to insure its survival (167).

78. Ibid., 169.

79. Dodge, "Living by Life," 5-12.

80. As one critiques Sale's model, it is well to bear in mind that "Marxists and capitalists agree on more than they disagree about: both see economic concerns as primary. Power is the highest good; law is an embodiment of power relations in a

society; those power relations are created by economics" (French, *Beyond Power*, 407).

81. Kirkpatrick Sale, *Dwellers in the Land: The Bioregional Vision* (San Francisco, Sierra Club Books: 1985), 51.

82. Ibid., 55.

83. Ibid., 55-62.

84. Ibid., 62-66. Sale also emphasizes the interdependence of these communities.

85. Ibid., 66. Sale notes that for the vast majority of "human time" we have lived as members of very small groups; the first city to reach one million was London in 1820 (63-64).

86. Ibid., 67-132. See page 50 for a chart which lists these attributes.

87. Ibid., 41-42.

88. Ibid., 42.

89. Ibid., 136. In regard to the past, Sale shows how bioregionalism is part of our American heritage, how there have always been those who, like Walt Whitman, have seen us as a "nation of nations" (136-49). He presents evidence that regionalism is a part of the present world situation, as seen, for example, in the increase of the number of nations in the U.N.; in the various separatist movements; in regionalism, which he defines as "the conscious breaking down of larger national structures into smaller and more manageable ones, and the self-conscious perception of differences of place" (157), whether in China, Russia, India, or the U.S.A. Office of Management and Budget (150-62). Bioregionalism presents a vision of the future that is not utopian but "doable" for these reasons: most people already see themselves as somehow related to a particular place; bioregionalism has the potential to attract a large constituency; it is a grassroots movement that only wants the federal government not to get in its way; it is already in process with more than sixty self-identified groups in place; it is already a national [in fact, an international] organization; it is part of the worldwide Green movement; it adheres to the virtues of gradualism (as opposed to revolution) and realism (163-79).

90. Bill Mollison, "Strategies for an Alternative Nation," in *Home!*, ed. Andruss, et al., 149-54. Mollison argues that we need to begin by stopping our dependence on far-away power structures, for it is in their interest to keep us helpless. Rather, we must identify where our resources are leaking from our self-identified bioregions, in the knowledge that we already have the technologies to solve our energy, food, and shelter problems. Mollison does not see this as isolationism because he sees natural and cultural linkages to exist among groups.

91. David Wheeler, "It All Comes Down to Earth" (Knoxville, TN: The Foundation for Global Sustainability, 1991). Wheeler defines *carrying capacity* as "the number of individuals of any species that can be maintained indefinitely in a given habitat area."

92. David Haenke's description of being led (as he and others were) to live in the Ozark bioregion, as well as the coming of many to this Congress, typify this experience of Spirit-led movement. Also see, C. T. Lawrence Butler, *On Conflict and Consensus* (Cambridge, MA: Food Not Bombs Publishing, 1987) for a "hands on" book on consensus decision-making.

I can attest to the fact that consensus decision-making does work—even in a group as emotionally charged as one on social justice in the 1960s. The bottom line seems to be the issue of good will.

93. Brian Tokar, *The Green Alternative: Creating an Ecological Future* (San Pedro: R. & E. Miles, 1987), 50.

94. Sale, *Dwellers in the Land*, 136.

95. Gene Marshall, "How Do We Get There from Here?" *Realistic Living: A Journal on Ethics and Religion* 15 (1992): 2-5. On these pages, Marshall is responding to Paul Shannon's analysis of the U.S.A. as coming out of a single center of power and for a need of a new center of power—a new center of gravity—to be developed if we are to transform the Earth. (see endnote 49 in this chapter.) Ultimately, Marshall thinks that only the building of new systems of culture, polity, and economics from the grassroots can call into being a "new center of gravity."

96. Berg, "Growing a Life-Place Politics," 143-44. Berg further notes that "ecological wisdom" is only one of the ten Green principles. And he contends that bioregionalists are more committed to "ecological wisdom" than are the Greens.

97. Capra and Spretnak, *Green Politics*, xix. This study is based largely, but not exclusively, on the then West German Greens.

98. Ibid., xx.

99. Spretnak, *The Spiritual Dimension of Green Politics*, 22-23.

100. Capra and Spretnak, *Green Politics*, 172-73.

101. Ibid., 178-79. The authors point out that this was possible in Belgium because of its representational system, where a percentage of the total vote entitles one to representatives. They contrast this to the winner-take-all system that exists in the U.S.A.

102. Tokar, *The Green Alternative*, 1.

103. Ibid., 1.

104. Capra and Spretnak, *Green Politics*, 29-47. For Tokar (*The Green Alternative*, 122-23), the principle of nonviolence is best symbolized by the women's Peace Camp at Greenham Common in Great Britain. He notes that when the Cruise missiles leave the base in their "secret" convoys, the women have the power to get this message out all over the world and have been known to stop the testing. On occasion, tens of thousands of women from all over Europe have come to Greenham to participate in the demonstrations.

105. Ibid., 47-49. One example of such a region would be comprised of the Allemannisch-speaking peoples of Germany, France, and Switzerland. This differs from the bioregionalism understanding of regions as keyed in the land itself.

106. Ibid., 49-53. Spretnak and Capra note that this value is not clearly lived out in, for example, their analyses, their actions, or the male/female ratio, especially at the national level.

107. Ibid., 53-56. Concern was also expressed about identifying spirituality and politics because of the way this was used by Hitler and his propagandists for their own ends.

108. Tokar, *The Green Alternative*, 34-44.

109. Ibid., 56.

110. Capra and Spretnak, *Green Politics*, 194-95. One might also contend that bioregionalism provides an example for the living out of this holistic vision.

111. Ibid., 196-99. Spretnak and Capra note that these lacks have kept women out of the Green party and have lessened the comprehensibility of the Greens' analysis of critical issues. They also stress that each country must develop its own unique Green party.

112. Ibid., xx-xxi. (This was written prior to the 1992 elections but I think it is

applicable in that instance also.) The Greens experience a problem from the political point of view in that the electoral districts and the bioregions are not comprised of the same areas.

113. Tokar, *The Green Alternative*, 137-47. Thus for example, people in the Berkshire Mountain bioregion (western Massachusetts) have created a community loan fund which encourages small alternative businesses. They are working to develop a local currency backed up by firewood. The monetary unit, the Berkshare, only circulates for one year, thus preventing hoarding and speculation. After one year, it may be traded in for dollars or new Berkshares. Many local merchants accept the local currency. These people, who are affiliated with the E.F. Schumacher Society, also have an expanding land trust (a non-profit organization which holds buildings and land in the name of the community rather than individuals) (110).

114. Ibid., 50-51. The Committees of Correspondence were created on a continent-wide basis in 1984, as was a national clearinghouse for Green resources based in Kansas City, Missouri.

115. Spretnak, *The Spiritual Dimension of Green Politics*, 77-82. One rich resource for the tenth value of "future focus" may be found in literature on feminist utopias. Sally Miller Gearhart examines eleven novels on feminist utopias from a political point of view. One of the issues she looks at is the relationship of these utopias to nature. She concludes that the novels contain several sound ecological principles such as the use of selective technology, empathetic relationships with animals, and responsible behavior in population control. See Sally Miller Gearhart, "Future Visions: Today's Politics: Feminist Utopias in Review," in *Women in Search of Utopias: Mavericks and Mythmakers*, ed. Ruby Rohrlich and Elaine Hoffman Baruch (New York: Schocken Books, 1984), 296-309.

116. Ibid., 27-38.

117. Ibid., 41-47. See Charlene Spretnak, *States of Grace: The Recovery of Meaning in the Postmodern Age* (San Francisco: Harper, 1991), for an expanded study on her understanding of some wisdom traditions as a basis for contemporary spirituality.

118. Ibid., 48-68. Thus, for the human person, postmodern religion would involve individual spiritual practice, community experiences such as weekly gatherings and annual retreats, and regular attention paid to spiritual moments such as those provided to us by our bodies; the human's relationship to the environment would celebrate our (Judaism's and Christianity's) connections with Nature and acknowledge our dependence on the "Old" Religion, and it would build on the churches' emerging stewardship program; our relationships to other people would be seen in terms of gender equality—in roles, in language, and in our imaging of the Divine—and through just structures on a global level for all marginalized groups.

119. Ibid., 71.

120. Ibid.

121. French, *Beyond Power*, 16.

4. Toward a Contemporary Cosmology

1. Carl Sagan, *Cosmos* (New York: Random House, 1980), 247.

2. Runes, ed., *The Dictionary of Philosophy*, 68. This definition is written by Paul Weiss.

3. Ibid., 69.

4. Ibid., 69.

5. Stephen W. Hawking, *A Brief History of Time: From the Big Bang to Black Holes* (Toronto: Bantam Books, 1988), vi.

6. While the elements I have chosen are the physical sciences, myth, mysticism, and theology, it is interesting to note the argument of Fatma Pinar Goktan Canevi that since Plato, but based on the pre-Socratics, the Western understanding of cosmology has consisted of two mutually incompatible elements – the myth of cosmogony (the story of the creation of the Universe) and the study of ontology (being as being). Canevi contends that this worked for Plato because he was able to combine the two in the poetry of *Timaeus*, but that we have given ourselves an impossible task in striving to combine these two elements. See, Fatma Pinar Goktan Canevi, "The Plight of Cosmology," *Process Studies* 17, no. 3 (Fall 1988): 163-69. It seems that the discoveries of the physical sciences have moved us into a new era for cosmology.

7. Gimbutas, *The Language of the Goddess*, xviii. Gimbutas bases her understanding of the function of myth on studies done by G. Dumézil (1898-1986).

8. French, *Beyond Power*, 49-54. In the social charter myth, French sees vestiges of a time when the female was powerful/good, while the transforming myths omit the past. As an example of a social charter myth with residual characteristics, French presents Eve and her association with the serpent (a symbol of regeneration) and with knowledge (knowledge which is forbidden by the new patriarchal god). Eve also presides over a garden of delights. As an example of a transformative myth, French presents Pandora, the bringer of all evil to humankind (it is not mentioned that her name means "giver of all gifts").

9. Ibid., 57-58.

10. Ibid., from *The Masks of God, Occidental Mythology* (New York: Penguin Books, 1976), 86.

11. Stone, *Ancient Mirrors of Womanhood*, 236.

12. Ibid., 362-66. While the Greek name for the Earth has become popularized as Gaia, it should be noted that according to Edith Hamilton, *Mythology* (Boston: Little, Brown and Company, 1963), the correct spelling is Gaea. The "G" is soft.

13. Ruby Rohrlich and June Nash, "Patriarchal Puzzle: State Formation in Mesopotamia and Mesoamerica," *Heresies 13, Earthkeeping/Earthshaking: Feminism and Ecology* 4, no. 1 (1981): 63. The authors note that Marduk defeats Tiamat, not because he is stronger, but because he has superior technology; that is, he is better armed. But they contend that the price men paid for this power over women lies in their complete servitude to earthly rulers.

14. French, *Beyond Power*, 271-72. French refers to this myth as one of male supremacy, but as such, she finds that it has a double bind. This double bind shows that in reality, man is utterly powerless for, on the one hand, he requires woman to mediate for him with nature while, on the other hand, he requires priests to mediate for him with God. In the former relationship, he must dominate; in the later relationship, he must be dominated. This leaves him in a position of being isolated as well as powerless. French notes further on that "it would not have been necessary to decree and impose inferiority on women if they were really inferior" (280). One could say that the myth was necessary to promote this world-view.

15. *Hindu Myths: A Sourcebook Translated from the Sanskrit*, introduction, Wender Doniger O'Flaherty (Great Britain: Penguin Books, 1976), 43.

16. Ibid., 345. The mathematics used for arriving at the duration of a *kalpa* may be found in, for example, *The Institutes of Vishnu*, trans. Julius Jolly (Delhi: Motilal Banarsidass, 1970), 77-78.

17. Sagan, *Cosmos*, 265-67. While citing the idea of the infinite number of universes as an old religious idea, he does not give the source for this citation (267). It is interesting to note that the four forces—which we will look at in the next section—almost seem to operate in different universes: the two nuclear in the very small, the electromagnetic in the intermediate, and gravity in the very large.

18. Fritjof Capra, *The Tao of Physics* (Boulder, CO: Shambhala, 1975), 25.

19. Ibid., 138. Some quantum theorists also suggest that scientists must be seen as participators rather than as observers. This is necessitated by their entering into the experiment and thereby making decisions which affect both scientists and the atomic particles they are trying to understand (140-42).

20. Ibid., 146-60.

21. Ibid., 161.

22. Ibid., 164-73.

23. Ibid., 189-99. Capra also notes that $E = mc^2$ has taught us a lesson in dynamism—that mass is simply a form of energy (200-203).

24. Ibid., 211.

25. Ibid., 207-11.

26. Ibid., 221-23.

27. Ibid., 224-44.

28. Ibid., 244-83. The quotation is from page 283.

29. Ibid., 291.

30. Ibid., 287. Capra goes on to note that, since this is not possible, scientists deal in approximations, which over time become more encompassing.

31. Ibid., 291.

32. Ibid., 286.

33. Ibid., 307.

34. David Maclagan, *Creation Myths: Man's Introduction to the World* (New York: Thames and Hudson, 1977), 5-7.

35. Ilya Prigogine and Isabelle Stengers, *Order Out of Chaos, Man's New Dialogue with Nature* (New York: Bantam, 1984), 121-22. The quotation is from page 122. Prigogine and Stengers work in terms of an entropy variation which is equal to the sum of the irreversible changes within a system and the changes which occur as a result of contact with the external environment (131). They view the unification of dynamics and thermodynamics as equivalent to the unification of being and becoming (255). Prigogine and Stengers see being and becoming as two aspects of the same reality, where initial conditions are associated with being and temporal changes with becoming. They also postulate the same kind of a paradigm for chance and necessity (255) and time and eternity (310).

36. Erich Jantsch, *The Self-Organizing Universe: Scientific and Human Implications of the Emerging Paradigm of Evolution* (Oxford: Pergamon Press, 1980), 8. He goes on to note that the positing of homologous principles overcomes the dualistic split between nature and culture in that all is a part of the dynamics of nature.

37. Stephen Toulmin, *The Return to Cosmology: Postmodern Science and the Theology of Nature* (Berkeley: University of California Press, 1982).

38. Ibid., 243.

39. Ibid., 249-50. According to Hawking, *A Brief History of Time*, 55, the uncer-

tainty principle is the basis for quantum mechanics. In quantum mechanics, one finds a prediction for a number of different possible outcomes and how likely each of these is.

40. Ibid., 250. These observations by Toulmin are found in a section of his book aptly entitled "Death of the Spectator," pp. 237-54.

41. Prigogine and Stengers, *Order Out of Chaos*, 217.

42. Ibid., 218.

43. Steven Weinberg, *The First Three Minutes: A Modern View of the Origin of the Universe* (New York: Basic Books, 1977), 4-5. The quotation is from page 5. Weinberg notes that the standard model of the Universe "may only describe a small part of the universe, or a limited portion of its history" (121).

44. Ibid., 5-6.

45. Ibid., 163. In cosmological terms, the red shift "refers to the observed shift of spectral lines of distant astronomical bodies toward long wavelengths." It grew out of an observation known as the Doppler effect, which one may observe on a highway or by a railroad by noticing how the engine of a fast-moving vehicle sounds higher pitched (has a shorter wavelength) when it is moving toward us than when it is moving away from us (12-14).

46. Ibid., 25-29. Weinberg points out that not everyone agrees with this interpretation of the red shift (28-29).

47. Ibid., 157. Black-body radiation is defined in Weinberg's glossary as "radiation with the same energy density in each wavelength range as the radiation emitted from a totally absorbing body. The radiation in any state of thermal equilibrium is black-body radiation."

48. Ibid., 44-76.

49. Ibid., 73. It should be noted here that some ecofeminists object to the birthing of the Universe being called the "Big Bang." For example, Starhawk, as cited by Brian Swimme, suggests that we should think of the beginning of the Universe as maternal: a birthing event. Swimme thinks the "Big Bang" terminology comes out of the fact that most physicists work on weapons' research, and that the facts of science, which are partial, need to be interpreted according to the vision of ecofeminism. As well as Starhawk's birthing event, he cites the image of mystery that weaves the Universe as seen by Charlene Spretnak. Brian Swimme, "How to Heal a Lobotomy," in *Reweaving the World*, ed. Diamond and Orenstein, 17-22.

50. Ibid., 102-6. Weinberg notes that there are at present two theories about the Universe before the first 1/100th of a second. One is based on a theory of "nuclear democracy," which posits a maximum temperature at which the energy density becomes infinite. The other is based on the "quark" theory, which posits a Universe possessing infinite density and infinite temperature. This is a Universe made up of free elementary particles. Both theories are associated with the strong nuclear force (137-42).

51. Ibid., 112.

52. Jantsch, *The Self-Organizing Universe*, 81-82. Prigogine and Stengers, *Order Out of Chaos*, 231, on whose theories Jantsch bases his work, posits a Universe born out of nonequalibrium and irreversible processes without which there would be no appreciable amount of matter but "only some fluctuating local excesses of matter over antimatter, or vice versa."

53. Bernard Lovell, *In the Center of Immensities* (New York: Harper & Row, 1978), 117-18, presents the four forces in the following way: the gravitational, which

is the concern of general relativity and determines the large scale nature of the Universe; the electromagnetic, which is evident in the interaction between two particles and is millions of times stronger than the gravitational force; the strong nuclear force, which binds protons and neutrons together in the atom and which, in the nucleus of the atom is 10^{40} times stronger than the gravitational force; the weak nuclear force, which is evident in atomic decay and is weaker than the electromagnetic force. The nuclear forces are explicable in terms of exchanges between fundamental particles. The gravitational force does not have a physical explanation except in terms of the hypothetical "graviton." In regard to the four forces, it should be noted that (Hawking, *A Brief History of Time*, 74-79) there presently exists what is called a Grand Unified Theory (GUT), which combines an understanding of the weak nuclear, strong nuclear, and electromagnetic fields. (It is neither "grand" nor fully unified, as it does not include the fourth force, gravity). It is based on an understanding that, at a very high energy level, the "three forces would all have the same strength and so could just be different aspects of a single force" (74). The experimental apparatus needed to test a GUT is formidable, but the theory has proven useful in possibly showing why there is matter in the Universe. Hawking is working toward a theory that would include gravity, a "quantum theory of gravity" (79ff.).

54. Hawking, *A Brief History of Time*, 116, theorizes that space-time is finite but has no boundary, that is, no beginning. He uses the analogy of the surface of the Earth but with two more dimensions. The Earth's surface is finite, but it has no boundaries—you can go around the Earth. If there is no boundary, there is no need to specify the behavior at the boundary, that is, at the moment of the Big Bang (135-36). "The universe would be completely self-contained and not affected by anything outside it. It would neither be created nor destroyed. It would just BE" (136).

55. Jantsch, *The Self-Organizing Universe*, 82-85.

56. Ibid., 85.

57. Ibid., 88-91. This principle of co-evolution is still in need of a unified theory to make it scientifically explicable. As Hawking, *A Brief History of Time*, 11-12, notes, at present two contradictory theories exist which partially explain the Universe's laws. They are the general theory of relativity, which applies to the large and super-large, and quantum mechanics, which works with phenomena of extremely small scales, for example, a millionth of a millionth inch. I would also note that according to Lovell (*In the Center of Immensities*, 5) classical science still works well in the intermediate range—the world we inhabit.

58. Ibid., 95-96.

59. Brian Swimme, "Canticle of the Cosmos" (from tape no. 1 of a twelve tape set of videos), Livermore, CA: The Tides Foundation, 1990.

60. Lovell, *In the Center of Immensities*, 70.

61. Jantsch, *The Self-Organizing Universe*, 88-89.

62. Lovell, *In the Center of Immensities*, 45.

63. Jantsch, *The Self-Organizing Universe*, 93.

64. Ibid., 12.

65. Lovell, *In the Center of Immensities*, 45-47.

66. Freeman Dyson, *Disturbing the Universe* (New York: Harper & Row, 1979), 250.

67. Ibid., 250-51.

68. Jantsch, *The Self-Organizing Universe*, 98.

69. Ibid., 110-20. As in the macrocosmos, Jantsch also finds symmetry breaks in the microcosmos. Time asymmetry occurs when the prokaryotes reproduce themselves, thereby enabling the transfer of vertical information. In other words, experience is no longer equivalent to present experience only; rather, experience from the past now also becomes a reality. Space asymmetry occurs when the eukaryotes (nucleated cells) develop sexuality, thereby enabling access to the experience of all the branches of the ancestral tree. These breaks occasioned an explosion in the forms of life (132-33).

70. J. E. Lovelock, *Gaia: A New Look at Life on Earth* (Oxford: Oxford University Press, 1979), ix.

71. Ibid., vii.

72. Ibid.

73. Ibid., 10.

74. Ibid., 19-25. Lovelock compares this to our body's ability to keep a constant temperature in summer's heat and winter's cold. As is the case in the maintenance of body temperature, he suggests that a number of processes such as controlling the amount of ammonia and increasing the heat absorption capability of the biosphere, were at work.

75. Ibid., 26.

76. Ibid., 35.

77. Ibid., 38.

78. Ibid., 49-50.

79. Ibid., 64-83.

80. Ibid., 86-100. An average sample of salt water contains 3.4 percent of inorganic salt per kilogram weight. Six percent would be fatal to almost all sea life, a significant loss since half the living beings on Earth live in the sea. The percentage of salt from the beginning of the oceans to the present has been kept stable.

81. Ibid., 146.

82. Ibid.

83. Ibid., 31.

84. Prigogine and Stengers, *Order Out of Chaos*, 9.

85. Ibid., 14.

86. Ibid., 178-79. A chemical clock refers to a far-from-equilibrium state in which all the molecules change their behavior at certain regular time intervals. This is one type of observable self-organization in nature. Critical to this behavior is the molecules' ability to communicate (147-48).

87. Ibid., 156-59.

88. Weinberg, *The First Three Minutes*, 150-51.

89. Lovell, *In the Center of Immensities*, 105-8. While these numbers do not add up as simple mathematics, given a Universe whose estimated age is ten to twenty billion years, this may be accounted for by Lovell's statement that the expanding and contracting phases of the Universe are not necessarily symmetrical (108).

90. Jantsch, *The Self-Organizing Universe*, 78. Citing Lloyd Motz, he puts the present period of pulsation at eighty billion years.

91. Weinberg, *The First Three Minutes*, 148-49. While a steady state model of the Universe may be a more philosophically satisfactory model, the evidence from the red shift and the background radiation has caused this model to be acceptable to few.

92. Lovell, *In the Center of Immensities*, 126.

93. Annie Dillard, *Pilgrim at Tinker Creek* (New York: Harper's Magazine Press, 1974), 204.

94. Capra, *The Tao of Physics*, 87.

95. Ruether, *New Woman, New Earth*, 194-95. Mircea Eliade, *The Sacred and the Profane* (New York: Harcourt, Brace and World, 1959), 107-9, suggests that it is only when the Cosmos is no longer seen as sacred that one experiences terror of cyclical views of time.

96. Jantzen, "Healing Our Brokenness," 133. It is interesting to note in this regard the insights of Jantsch, not a theologian but a scientist and a philosopher, that true creativity lies in our ability to overcome the dualism between the creator and the created (Jantsch, *The Self-Organizing Universe*, 17).

97. Ibid., 133-35.

98. Ibid., 137.

99. Maclagan, *Creation Myths*, 13-14, offers the interesting suggestion that chaos is a state where everything is, but nothing is differentiated. His description sounds very much like the state of the Universe during the first micro-second.

100. Jantzen, "Healing Our Brokenness," 132.

101. Jantzen, *God's World, God's Body*, 131.

102. Ibid., 135. Jantzen sees Creation as involving a relationship of everlasting ontological dependence (140).

103. Ibid. Jantzen does this using throughout the book a non-dualistic model of the human person as an analogy for the World-God relationship. However, she cites as a "dis-analogy" the fact that God is more totally embodied than we are. Everything is subject to God's volition (143).

104. Ibid., 74-85.

105. Ibid., 85-93.

106. Ibid., 93-100.

107. Ibid., 149.

108. Ibid., 152.

109. Ibid., 122-30.

110. Starhawk, "Feminist Earth-based Spirituality and Ecofeminism" in *Healing the Wounds*, ed. Plant, 177-78. Of course, Starhawk and the *Baltimore Catechism* express the Divine embodiment differently: the former in terms of the immanence of the Goddess, and the latter in terms of God's being everywhere.

111. Brian Swimme, *The Universe Is a Green Dragon: A Cosmic Creation Story* (Santa Fe, NM: Bear & Company, 1985), 146. This understanding of creation also seems to be expressed by Aquinas when he says that "The act of the Father's begetting the Son and the Father's creating the world is one and the same." Thomas Aquinas, *Summa Theologica* I. q. 34, a.3.

112. Jürgen Moltmann, "The Scope of Renewal in the Spirit," *The Ecumenical Review* 42:2 (1990):101. He goes on to say that God's true temple is the Cosmos itself: "Essentially the church is cosmically orientated. . . . The nihilistic destruction of nature is applied atheism" (102).

113. Moltmann, *God in Creation*, 154. While the spelling of Shekhina and Kabbala vary in the sources, I have chosen to use one form only for the sake of consistency.

114. Rae and Marie-Daly, *Created in Her Image*, 12-13.

115. Berry, *The Dream of the Earth*, 120.

116. Swimme, *The Universe Is a Green Dragon*, 38-39.

117. Berry, *The Dream of the Earth*, 20.

118. Thomas Berry, "The Earth: A New Context for Religious Unity," in *Thomas Berry and the New Cosmology*, ed. Anne Lonergan and Caroline Richards (Mystic, CT: Twenty-Third Publications, 1988), 37.

119. Ibid., 38.

120. Berry, *The Dream of the Earth*, 81. On this same theme Susan Griffin, "Curves Along the Road," in *Reweaving the World*, ed. Diamond and Orenstein, 87, makes the telling comment that it is the material of our bodies which is immortal; at death, the form changes.

121. For a perceptive and concise summary of the science-religion controversy and its implications, as well as the reasons why the separation is lessening today, see Rosemary Radford Ruether, *Gaia and God: An Ecofeminist Theology of Earth Healing* (San Francisco: Harper, 1992), 32-38.

122. Capra, *The Tao of Physics*, 20.

123. Berry, *The Dream of the Earth*, 132.

124. Mary Southard, "Spiritearth" 2, no. 1 (1991):1. See Southard for a beautiful expression of Berry's New Story through the medium of painting.

125. Swimme, *The Universe Is a Green Dragon*, 39-40.

126. Thomas Berry, "Our Future on Earth: Where Do We Go From Here?," in *Thomas Berry and the New Cosmology*, ed. Lonergan and Richards, 104.

127. Berry, *The Dream of the Earth*, 131-32. Berry expands on this theme in the following words: "Neither humans as a species nor any of our activities can be understood in any significant manner except in our role in the functioning of the earth and of the universe itself. We come into existence, have our present meaning, and attain our destiny within this numinous context, for the universe in its every phase is numinous in its depths, is relevatory in its functioning, and in its human expression finds its fulfillment in celebratory self-awareness" (87).

128. Swimme, *The Universe Is a Green Dragon*, 87.

129. Ibid., 87-88.

130. Ibid., 43-52. Berry, *The Dream of the Earth*, 20, finds in the Asian world terms of cosmic significance that signify supremely affectionate qualities. These include the Chinese *jen* (love, affection, benevolence); the Indian *bhakti* (devotional love); and the Buddhist *karuna* (compassion).

131. Ibid., 88-95.

132. Ibid., 102.

133. Ibid., 99-109.

134. Ibid., 113-23.

135. Ibid., 127-39.

136. Ibid., 143-51.

137. Ibid., 147.

138. Hawking, *A Brief History of Time*, 140-41.

139. Moltmann, *God in Creation*, 153-56.

140. Prigogine and Stengers, *Order Out of Chaos*, 176.

5. The Holy Spirit as the Feminine Divine

1. Yves Congar, *I Believe in the Holy Spirit*, vol. 3 (New York: The Seabury Press, 1983), 155.

2. Rae and Marie-Daly, *Created in Her Image*. See especially 19-22.

3. See, for example, Linda A. Mercadante, *Gender, Doctrine & God: The Shakers and Contemporary Theology* (Nashville: Abingdon Press, 1990) for a well-researched and well-written example of a religious sect where a change in the status of women preceded a change in the Divine language and symbol system.

4. I agree with Rosemary Ruether "that merely replacing a male transcendent deity with an immanent female one is an insufficient answer to the 'god-problem.' " (*Gaia and God*, 4). Rather, what I see as needed is a model of the Divinity which adequately addresses both the female and the male aspects of the Divine. The beginnings for this model may be found in my proposed trinitarian construct (see pp. 89-90 above).

5. Donald L. Gelpi, *Divine Mother: A Trinitarian Theology of the Holy Spirit* (Lanham, MD: University Press of America, 1984), 140.

6. I am comfortable neither with the word *gender* nor with the word *sex* in regard to the femininity of the Holy Spirit. However, I do not know an alternative word that would be more appropriate. I do find of value here Lerner's distinction between sex and gender. She sees sex as that which distinguishes women as "a separate group due to their biological distinctiveness ... Gender is the cultural definition of behavior defined as appropriate to the sexes in a given society at a given time" (Lerner, *The Creation of Patriarchy*, 238). In other words, sex is biological while gender is cultural. Obviously, the Holy Spirit is determined neither by biology nor by culture.

7. See for example, Leonardo Boff, *Trinity and Society* (Maryknoll, NY: Orbis Books, 1989), 182, who sees femininity as a basic constituent of the male as well as the female. For Boff, femininity encompasses "tenderness, care, self-acceptance, mercy, sensitivity to the mystery of life and of God, cultivation of the interiority that does and must exist in any human life that has reached a minimum level of maturity."

8. Edward O'Connor, "The Spirit in Catholic Thought," in *God, Jesus, and Spirit*, ed. Daniel Callahan (New York: Herder and Herder, 1969), 246.

9. This Assembly took place in Canberra, Australia, in February of 1991. While I played a small part in the pre-Assembly work and found it very worthwhile, I am not sure what effect the Assembly itself had on the WCC. It does seem safe to say that no major breakthroughs were made in regard to a much needed theology of the Holy Spirit. But theology is not the work of assemblies.

10. Rae and Marie-Daly, *Created in Her Image*, 26-28.

11. I understand Spirit and Wisdom as representing the same aspect of the feminine Divine in the writings of the Hebrew scriptures. This view is also articulated, for example, in Kathleen M. O'Connor, *The Wisdom Literature* (Wilmington, DE: Michael Glazier, 1988), 178; and Congar, *I Believe in the Holy Spirit* I, 9. We will look at this issue in more depth when we look at the person of the Holy Spirit in the final section of this chapter.

12. George T. Montague, *The Holy Spirit: Growth of a Biblical Tradition* (New York: Paulist Press, 1976), 106.

13. O'Connor, *The Wisdom Literature*, 84.

14. Ibid., 83-84.

15. Leonardo Boff, *The Maternal Face of God: The Feminine and Its Religious Expressions* (San Francisco: Harper & Row, 1987).

16. Boff, *Trinity and Society*, 210-12.

17. Ibid., 212.

18. Jantsch, *The Self-Organizing Universe*, 17.

19. It is interesting to note that James H. Charlesworth, "Explorations: Rethinking Relationships Among Jesus and Christians" 6, no. 1 (1992): 4, cites a Jewish-Christian audience with John Paul II, who stated that "every authentic prayer is called forth by the Holy Spirit, who is mysteriously present in the heart of every person."

20. I have used this understanding of Luke 7:35 on a number of occasions, suggesting, for example, that it be incorporated into a paper I helped prepare for the WCC Pre-Assembly Consultation: "Giver of Life—Sustain Your Creation," Petaling Jaya, Malaysia, May 12-21, 1990. In this instance it was rejected for inclusion in the paper by a prominent scripture scholar. While continuing to use this interpretation, I appreciated hearing reinforcement for my insight given in a paper presented at the annual meeting of the Society of Biblical Literature, November 22, 1992. In his paper entitled "Yet Wisdom Is Justified by Her Children: A Rhetorical and Compositional Analysis of Divine Sophia in Q," Patrick John Hartin's points included the following: that for the Q community, John and Jesus are both children of the Divine Sophia; that they are the ones of their own generation to whom the Divine Sophia has communicated Herself; that as Her children, they are called upon to justify Her; that the importance of Jesus lies in his role as spokesperson of Sophia—that is to say, in his words and not in his death and resurrection.

21. Gelpi, *The Divine Mother*, 65.

22. The reader is referred to Rae and Marie-Daly, *Created in Her Image*, 24-26, for a prior discussion on the issue of the Spirit/Word relationship.

23. Congar, *I Believe in the Holy Spirit*, 3:155.

24. Moltmann, "The Scope of Renewal in the Spirit," 101.

25. Montague, *The Holy Spirit*, 70.

26. Ibid., 30-31.

27. Ibid., 42-44.

28. Ibid., 85-87.

29. Ibid., 49-50.

30. Congar, *I Believe in the Holy Spirit*, 1:29.

31. Ibid., 37.

32. Ibid., 37-39. While some theologians argue that Paul does not distinguish the Risen Christ and the Holy Spirit, Congar does not agree. To substantiate his position he cites, for example, 2 Corinthians 3:16-17, which refers to the Spirit of the Lord. However, he does note that there is no dogmatic statement in Paul on the Trinity as three and yet one (39).

33. Ibid., 55-56.

34. Yves Congar, *Tradition and Traditions* (New York: Macmillan, 1967), 374.

35. Boff, *The Maternal Face of God*.

36. Rae and Marie-Daly, *Created in Her Image*, 89-90. On this issue it is interesting to note that Alasdair Heron, "The Filioque in Recent Reformed Theology," in *Spirit of God, Spirit of Christ: Ecumenical Reflections on the Filioque Controversy*, ed. Lukas Vischer (London: SPCK, 1981), 111, states that Karl Barth defended the *filioque* because it was "a barrier blocking the road to any kind of access to the Father otherwise than through Jesus Christ." The quotation is from *Church Dogmatics* I/1, no.12, 2.3 (Edinburgh: T. & T. Clark, 1975), 481. From the point of view

of the Holy Spirit, it must be said that the *filioque* clause stands against Her mission as universal bestower of salvation.

37. Gelpi, *The Divine Mother*, 133. Gelpi articulates six other theological ways of understanding the triunity: modalism, reduction to mystery, substantial unity, dynamic vitalism, mutual inexistence, and tritheism. Some, such as modalism and tritheism, are considered heretical. Gelpi sees dynamic vitalism (Gaius Marius Victorinus) and mutual inexistence (John of Damascus) as offering the best possibilities for today's theologians (127-33).

38. Ibid., 133-35.

39. Ibid., 135-36. Gelpi also cites John of Damascus and his use of *perichoresis* as being the equivalent of their unity rather than a consequence of that unity (132). This same idea of the mutual interpenetration of two realities which remain nevertheless distinct is also a human experience. Or, as Gelpi sees it, we do not have experiences; we each are an experience. "The persons and things that have changed me have become part of me, flesh of my flesh, love of my love, just as I in changing them have become part of them" (42). Because I am an experience, not only do I exist in my world, but my world exists in me (41-42).

40. Ibid., 136.

41. Ibid., 45-60. Justin Martyr (c. 100-c. 165) diverged from biblical Pneumatology in that he equated the Divine intelligence with the Son as well as the Spirit. For Clement of Alexandria (c. 159-c. 215), there was only one principle of enlightenment, the Son. Basically, this path, where the *Logos* and not the Spirit came to be seen as the Divine intelligence, is the path followed by Origen, Augustine, and Aquinas (61-63).

42. Ibid., 64-65.

43. Ibid., 217. See 217-18 for the actual quotation from Victorinus on which Gelpi bases his statement. This does not create problems for seeing Mary as the Mother of the Divinity if one sees her as incarnating the Holy Spirit.

44. Ibid., 138. It would not be said that He proceeds from Her, as She does not generate Him as efficacious cause, as does the Father.

45. Ibid., 232-33. Gelpi's commentary on Victorinus also includes the following: Jesus as androgynous is characterized by his capacity to reconcile both great strength and great gentleness in his dealings with others; that masculinity is a part — a sign — and not the whole; that Jesus is also the Christ and we who are his mystical body are part of the Christ.

46. Ibid., 45. Can we also say that we experience Jesus as the One who does the will of the Holy One because it is through him that we experience the Holy Spirit as Wisdom and the first person of the Trinity as Mother?

47. Ibid., 45-60.

48. Ibid., 60. Gelpi traces the loss of the biblical understanding of the Holy Spirit though the theologizing of the apostolic fathers, the church apologists, Augustine, Ambrose, and Aquinas (60-63).

49. Ibid., 5. Augustine's theology followed this path of ascribing enlightenment to the Word. Rather than as enlightenment, he saw the Spirit as Love. Gelpi sees the scripture as ascribing both enlightenment and love to the Spirit; love is a way of knowing (141). I ask: Can one equate a concept, for example, love, with a personal Divinity? Rather than being the totality of the Person, must it not be viewed as a quality the Spirit manifests?

50. Ibid., 215-32.

51. Ibid., 47. It has been suggested that in the world religions (source unknown) there are two ways to salvation: the way of the kitten and the way of the monkey. In the way of the kitten, when danger comes, the mother cat takes the kitten up in her mouth and carries her to safety (Christ?). In the way of the monkey, when dangers comes, the mother monkey rushes to safety and it is the task of the baby monkey to jump on her back as she is rushing by (the Spirit?).

52. Ibid., 71.

53. Boff, *Trinity and Society*, 170-71. It should be noted that in his Trinitarian theology Boff emphasized *perichoresis* rather than monarchy.

54. Ibid., 146-47.

55. However, that Boff is looking for mutuality and not domination may be seen from the following quotation:

> Trinitarian communion is a source of inspiration rather than of criticism in the social sphere. Christians committed to social change based in the needs of majorities, above all, see tri-unity as their permanent utopia. The three "Differents" uphold their difference one from another; by upholding the other and giving themselves totally to the other, they become "Differents" in communion. In the Trinity there is no domination by one side, but convergence of the Three in mutual acceptance and giving. They are different but none is greater or lesser, before or after. Therefore a society that takes its inspiration from trinitarian communion cannot tolerate class differences, dominations based on power (economic, sexual or ideological) that subjects those who are different to those who exercise that power and marginalizes the former from the latter.
>
> The sort of society that would emerge from inspiration by the trinitarian model would be one of fellowship, equality of opportunity, generosity in the space available for personal and group expression. Only a society of sisters and brothers whose social fabric is woven out of participation and communion of all in everything can justifiably claim to be an image and likeness (albeit pale) of the Trinity, the foundation and final resting-place of the universe (Boff, *Trinity and Society*, 151).

56. Jean-Miguel Garrigues, "A Roman Catholic View of the Position Now Reached in the Question of the Filioque," in *Spirit of God, Spirit of Christ*, ed. Vischer, 157. It should be noted that the phrase "through the Son" is the wording used, for example, by the Council of Florence (1439).

57. See Rae and Marie-Daly, *Created in Her Image*, 87-89, for a discussion of the use of *Abba* in the Jewish and Christian traditions.

58. Garrigues, "A Roman Catholic View," 159.

59. Boris Bobrinskoy, "The Filioque Yesterday and Today," in *Spirit of God, Spirit of Christ*, ed. Vischer, 145.

60. Boff, *Trinity and Society*, 194. This understanding of the Spirit is elaborated on in pages 194-96.

61. Moltmann, *God in Creation*, 281. In the blessing of the Sabbath, Moltmann sees, not a blessing of Creation, but a blessing of time. The blessing of the Sabbath is not a blessing of activity but the Divinity's gift of Presence.

62. Gelpi, *The Divine Mother*, 105-9. See pages 103-4 for a summary statement

on the development of the word *person* as a proper term for theologizing, not explicitly about the Holy Spirit, but in a Trinitarian context.

63. Ibid., 111-14. In our own time, theologians such as Heribert Mühlen and Jürgen Moltmann make explicit use of the term *person* in their theologizing; for different reasons, there is expressed hesitancy on the part of Karl Barth and Karl Rahner, for example, to employ this term (103 and 110-11).

64. Boff, *Trinity and Society*, 10.

65. Boff, *The Maternal Face of God*, 123-76. Referring to the altar at Isenheim, Dr. Susenne Schaup, Munich, Germany, in a letter to me dated October 5, 1993, gave the following observation:

I wonder if you have seen a photograph of those mysterious female figures above the "concert of angels?" There are, as a matter of fact, seven of them within that blue aureole, and there are some more outside. Most of them might be classified as angels. But the central one has golden flames springing from her forehead. Her hands are folded, and her long wavy hair and soft face seem to identify her as a female figure. She is the one most often interpreted as Sophia, Divine Wisdom, before she incarnates as Mary, as she is seen in the next segment of the tabernacle image. Here, Mary wears a crown that looks like golden-red flames. Some (men) have interpreted the central figure in the aureole as Hermes Trismegistus, but I think this is wrong. Now, directly behind the figure with the flaming forehead is a blue figure, without wings, with upper body and arms delineated. Her face is turned upward and wears a look of strange longing or yearning. I take her to be Uncreated Sophia, the divine idea of Her, if you will, before she turns into the lady with the flaming head.

66. O'Connor, *The Wisdom Literature*. The Wisdom literature is comprised of Proverbs, Job, Ecclesiastes, and part of Psalms (for Catholics, Jews, and Protestants). Also, for Roman Catholics and Greek Jews only, it includes the Book of Sirach and the Wisdom of Solomon (22).

67. Ibid., 23-28.

68. Ibid., 19-21. For O'Connor, the Wisdom literature sees holiness in terms of relationships. It contains four major themes that are pertinent for today:
1. It sees confusion and ambiguity as a way of breakthrough to transcendent mystery.
2. It sees that evil sometimes annihilates good and asks how this can be if there is a just God.
3. It uses feminine words and symbols for the Divine, for example, *Hokmah* (wisdom).
4. It offers a theology of community.

69. Susan Cady, Marian Ronan, and Hal Taussig, *Sophia: The Future of Feminist Spirituality* (San Francisco: Harper & Row, 1986), 22-23. The authors also cite Proverbs 1:20-22 and Proverbs 8:1-11 as texts which speak to the issue of the need to learn (22).

70. Ibid., 22.

71. Ibid., 24-26.

72. Ibid., 26.

73. O'Connor, *The Wisdom Literature*, 34.

74. Ibid., 72.

75. Ibid., 83-84.

76. Montague, *The Holy Spirit*, 50.

77. Ibid., 103-4.

78. Ibid., 106.

79. O'Connor, *The Wisdom Literature*, 178. On page 112 of the Apocrypha of the *Oxford Annotated Bible*, ed. Herbert G. May and Bruce M. Metzger (New York: Oxford University Press, 1965), this identification of Wisdom with the Holy Spirit is also made.

80. See Rae and Marie-Daly, *Created in Her Image*, 16-22, for a description of why this tradition was lost to us as well as a rationale for why this tradition must be rediscovered.

6. The Feminine in the Major World Religions

1. Paul R. Fries, "Incandescence: Three Meditations on the Holy Spirit," *Perspectives: A Journal of Reformed Thought* 4, no. 8 (1989): 6.

2. One from many possible examples is the conference held at Hartford Seminary on November 6-7, 1992, on Native American spirituality. Workshops and ritualizing were presented by members of the tribal peoples — many from the local area.

3. Young, "Introduction," in *Women in World Religions*, ed. Sharma, 7.

4. Stone, *Ancient Mirrors of Womanhood*, 211-12. The Harappan culture flourished about 3000 B.C.E., spreading out about 950 miles along the Indus River and its tributaries. A vast number of Goddess statues have been found, "many quite similar to those found in Mesopotamia" (212). The second and later strain that confronted this culture and became a part of Hinduism — comes from the lighter skinned Aryan invaders, who began their invasions in about 2000 B.C.E. and brought with them their trinity of male gods: Indra, Mitra and Varuna.

5. Eck, *Darśan*, 24.

6. Samuel Rayan, "Naming the Unnamable," in *Naming God*, ed. Robert P. Scharlemann (New York: Paragon House, 1985), 10.

7. Stone, *Ancient Mirrors of Womanhood*, 214.

8. Ibid., 211.

9. Tracy Pintchman, "Deciphering the Goddess: The Feminine Principle in Brahmanical Hindu Cosmogony and Cosmology." Ph.D. diss. Santa Barbara: University of California, 1992: 72.

10. Shiva, *Staying Alive*, 40.

11. Ibid., 40-41.

12. Pupul Jayakar, *The Earth Mother: Legends, Goddesses, and Ritual Arts of India* (San Francisco: Harper & Row, 1990), 14.

13. Ibid., 10-14.

14. Ibid., 182-83.

15. Ibid., xii.

16. Ibid., 192.

17. Ibid., xii.

18. Ibid., 17. As such, She would seem to correspond to stage one of Campbell's four stages of the Goddess. With Her rediscovery, it may be postulated that we are

entering stage five, where both the Feminine — and the Masculine — Principles, will be equally honored.

19. Ibid., xiii.

20. Ibid., 17.

21. Ibid., xiii.

22. Ibid., 21-23. It is noteworthy that this geometric motif is also apparent in the ritualistic fires used in Hindu worship. The private fires are circular and represent the Earth and this World; the public are rectangular and represent the sky and the other World. Nirad C. Chaudhuri, *Hinduism: A Religion to Live By* (New York: Oxford University Press, 1979), 77-79, further notes that this was also true for the ancient Romans, where the eternal private fire of the nation was attended by the Vestal Virgins.

23. Ibid., 183-84.

24. Ibid., 34-36.

25. Chaudhuri, *Hinduism*, 46.

26. Stone, *Ancient Mirrors of Womanhood*, 211-13.

27. Jayakar, *The Earth Mother*, 46.

28. Ibid., 46-47.

29. Lina Gupta, "Kali, the Savior," in *After Patriarchy: Feminist Transformations of the World Religions*, ed. Paula M. Cooey, William R. Eakin, Jay B. McDaniel (Maryknoll, NY: Orbis Books, 1991), 15. Kali's dark complexion possibly indicates her link to the indigenous fertility goddess as well as to the Earth (22).

30. Ibid., 15. In transcending, one must ask what happens to the needs of women which are satisfied by the Great Mother and the Earth, which has traditionally been seen as feminine.

31. Ibid., 25-29. While the spelling of Śakti and prakrti is not uniform in the sources used, I have chosen to use one form for the sake of the reader. This is also true for Śiva which occurs later in this section.

32. Ibid., 31-37.

33. Jayakar, *The Earth Mother*, 53.

34. Wendy O'Flaherty, trans., *The Rig Veda* (New York: Penguin Books, 1981), 38.

35. Pintchman, "Deciphering the Goddess," 222.

36. Ibid., 223.

37. Ibid., 223-24.

38. Ibid., 226. Pintchman notes that the *Purānas* which depict the Goddess as the Absolute are all classified as minor rather than major.

39. Ibid., 228-29.

40. Shiva, *Staying Alive*, 38-39. On these same pages, Shiva identifies a third principle — *Purusha* — the Masculine Principle with whom *Prakriti* creates the world. Further, she speaks of *Prakriti* as being the masculine and feminine manifestation of *Śakti*, the primordial feminine energy.

41. Ibid., 39.

42. Ibid.

43. Wendell Charles Beane, *Myth, Cult and Symbols in Śakta Hinduism* (Leiden: E. J. Brill, 1977), 37.

44. Ibid., 41.

45. Ibid., 42-149. The Hindu understanding of Brahmā is as a creator god, while Brahman is understood as the Absolute Ultimate beyond all gods. In his

writing, Beane seems to be saying that the Goddess, as both immanent and transcendent, replaces both Brahmā and Brahman in *Śākta* Hinduism.

46. Ibid., 150-52.

47. Ibid., 155-56. The quotation is from page 156.

48. Ibid., 169-71.

49. Ibid., 174-80. The quotation is from page 180.

50. Ibid., 181.

51. Ibid., 163.

52. Ibid.

53. Ibid., 260.

54. Jayakar, *The Earth Mother*, 84. The line cited features Pāndu speaking to Kuntī.

55. Ibid., 15.

56. Ibid., 183-84.

57. Gupta, "Kali the Savior," in *After Patriarchy*, ed. Cooey, et al., 16.

58. Ibid., 17-20.

59. Stone, *Ancient Mirrors of Womanhood*, 213-14. Also note the previously cited article by Wulff, "Images and Roles of Women," in which she finds evidence for the positive correlation between the social status of women in Bengal and the worship of the Goddess to be strong, but not conclusive.

60. Young, "Introduction," in *Women in World Religions*, ed. Sharma, 28.

61. Beane, *Myth, Cult and Symbols*, 266-68.

62. Ibid., 167.

63. Raphael Patai, *The Hebrew Goddess* (Detroit: Wayne State University, 1990), 29.

64. Ibid., 152. This term, Matronit-Shekhina, is used by Patai because, while the mysticism of the Kabbala that developed in revitalized form beginning in the thirteenth century still employed the term Shekhina, the term Matronit was also used to indicate the Feminine Divine's new and high status (32).

65. Ibid., 63.

66. Ibid., 52-53.

67. Savina J. Teubal, *Sarah the Priestess: The First Matriarch of Genesis* (Athens, OH: Swallow Press, 1984).

68. Ibid., 102-3. Teubal further notes that while the priestesses of the Near East were to remain childless, it was possible that they might conceive, presumably during the rite of the *hieras gamos* (sacred marriage). A child so conceived was to be exposed to the elements. Could the binding of Isaac have its origin in this tradition? (82-83).

69. The need for such a role model may be seen as a corrective to the role given to women in a monotheistic culture, according to the analysis of Judith Ochshorn, *The Female Experience and the Nature of the Divine* (Bloomington: Indiana University, 1981), 226.

> Both testaments introduced, in a systemic way, the concept of a secular hierarchy based on sex, in which power and powerlessness became associated with gender; virtue and honor came to mean different things for each sex; and men came to be seen in their secular roles as the more authentic spokesmen for the divine, at the same time that women were portrayed in a variety of roles in the community of believers and were both honored and valued in

some of them. In short, it was both the monotheistic elevation of the importance of gender as the basis of power and the ambivalence exhibited toward women as a sex that were most alien, in many respects, to the vision and practices of polytheistic religions in the ancient Near East.

70. Cady, et al., *Sophia*, 74-75.

71. John Eaton, *The Contemplative Face of Old Testament Wisdom: In the Context of World Religions* (London: SCM Press, 1989), 13.

72. Cady, et al., *Sophia*, 80-86.

73. Patai, *The Hebrew Goddess*, 165. See page 153 for an expansion for how the Matronit—*Shekhina* satisfies this psychological need for the male.

74. Ibid., 192.

75. Ibid., 279.

76. Susannah Heschel, "Feminism," in *Contemporary Jewish Religious Thought: Original Essays on Critical Concepts, Movements, and Beliefs*, ed. Arthur A. Cohen and Paul Mendes-Flohr (New York: Charles Scribner's Sons, 1987), 256-57. Heschel sees in the writings of feminists such as Savina Teubal and Jane Litman an argument that the biblical and talmudic sources contain hints of "a vibrant tradition of women's spirituality eventually excluded from the mainstream of Jewish religion" (257-58).

77. Judith Plaskow, "The Right Question is Theological," in *On Being a Jewish Feminist: A Reader*, ed. Susannah Heschel (New York: Schocken Books, 1983), 223-33.

78. Judith Plaskow, *Standing Again at Sinai: Judaism from a Feminist Perspective* (San Francisco: Harper & Row, 1990), 122. See pages 123-34 for a discussion of God as male and as dominating Other.

79. Ibid., 127-28.

80. Ibid., 138.

81. Ibid., 139-40. Arthur Green, "Bride, Spouse, Daughter: Images of the Feminine in Classical Jewish Sources," in *On Being a Jewish Feminist*, ed. Heschel, 248-49, also questions the usefulness to women of feminine images created by males. In this same article, he speaks of the need men have for feminine images in regard to their own spiritual wholeness.

82. Ibid., 140-45.

83. Ibid., 161-64.

84. Ibid., 146.

85. Ibid., 148-51.

86. Ibid., 167-68.

87. Rita M. Gross, "Female God Language in a Jewish Context," in *Womanspirit Rising: A Feminist Reader in Religion*, ed. Carol P. Christ and Judith Plaskow (San Francisco: Harper & Row, 1979), 173. She argues that because Judaism is theistic, personal language and images are needed by definition, and that these images and words must be feminine as well as masculine (167-73).

88. Rita Gross, "Steps Toward Feminine Imagery of Deity in Jewish Theology," in *On Being a Jewish Feminist*, ed. Heschel, 242-47.

89. Chava Weissler, "For Women and for Men Who Are Like Women: The Construction of Gender in Yiddish Devotional Literature," *Journal of Feminist Studies in Religion* 5:2 (1989):21. This quotation is from the *Tklaine imrei Shifre*, attributed to Shifrah, a woman from Poznan, and is dated some time after 1770 (19-20).

90. Adelman, "New Rituals, Ancient Traditions," *Woman of Power*, 19 (1991): 30.

91. Cited by Plaskow, *Standing Again at Sinai*, 237.

92. Carol Christ, "Woman's Liberation and the Liberation of God: An Essay in Story Theology," in *The Jewish Woman: New Perspectives*, ed. Elizabeth Koltun (New York: Schocken Books, 1976), 11-17.

93. Cynthia Ozick, "Notes Toward Finding the Right Question," in *On Being a Jewish Feminist*, ed. Heschel, 120-22.

94. Ibid., 142-51.

95. Plaskow, *Standing Again at Sinai*, 236.

96. Naomi Goldenberg, *Changing of the Gods: Feminism and the End of Traditional Religions* (Boston: Beacon Press, 1979), 63.

97. Ibid., 63-64.

98. Ibid., 84.

99. Ibid., 89.

100. Ibid., 120.

101. Ibid.

102. Ibid., 125-26.

103. Ibid., 128-40.

104. Plaskow, *Standing Again at Sinai*, 218-19.

105. Ibid., 231-32.

106. Young, "Introduction," in *Women in World Religions*, ed. Sharma, 7.

107. Jack Kornfield, "Is Buddhism Changing in North America?," in *Buddhist America: Centers, Retreats, Practices*, ed. Don Morreale (Santa Fe: John Muir Publications, 1988), xxvi.

108. Ibid., xiv-xv.

109. Diana Paul, *Women in Buddhism: Images of the Feminine in Mahāyāna Tradition* (Berkeley: University of California, 1985), xxiv-xxv.

110. Ibid., xxv-xxvii.

111. Ibid., 281-85.

112. Ibid., 287.

113. Ibid., 166-70.

114. Ibid., 170.

115. Ibid., 170-71.

116. Ibid., 177-79. These four stories, including commentary, may be found on pages 180-211 of *Women in Buddhism*.

117. Ibid., 217-41.

118. Ibid., 288-89.

119. Ibid., 247-49.

120. Ibid., 250.

121. Ibid., 250-52. In her keynote address at the Seventh Assembly of the World Council of Churches, held in Canberra, Australia, February 8, 1991, Korean Theologian Chung Hyun-Kyung showed a slide of Kuan-yin, who she said was her image of the Holy Spirit. She noted that Kuan-yin refuses to enter Nirvana until she can take the whole universe—people, trees, mountains, air, water, birds—with her. "Come, Holy Spirit, Renew the Whole Creation," video tape available from Lou Niznik, 15726 Ashland Dr., Laurel, MD 20707. See Mary Evelyn Tucker, "Expanding Contexts, Breaking Boundaries: The Challenge of Chung Hyun-Kyung," *Cross Currents* (Summer, 1992): 236-43, for a perceptive and knowledgeable article on

Chung's talk. She suggests that the talk may be seen not in terms of syncretism but rather in terms of enculturation. As an East Asian feminist theologian, Chung drew on elements from Shamanism, Confucianism, and Buddhism, as well as the Western Christianity in which she has been educated.

122. C. N. Tay, "Kuan-Yin: The Cult of Half Asia," in *History of Religions* 16, no. 2 (1976): 153-54.

123. Ibid., 171.

124. Joanna Macy, "Perfection of Wisdom: Mother of All Buddhas," in *Beyond Androcentrism: New Essays on Women and Religion*, ed. Rita M. Gross (Missoula, MT: Scholars Press, 1977), 315.

125. Ibid., 316-20. The quotation is from page 320.

126. Ibid., 322.

127. Ibid., 324-25.

128. Ibid., 330.

129. Stephanie Kaza, "Acting with Compassion: Buddhism, Feminism, and the Environmental Crisis," in *Ecofeminism and the Sacred*, ed. Carol J. Adams, (New York: Continuium, 1993), 50-51. The quotation is from page 51.

130. China Galland, *Longing for Darkness: Tara and the Black Madonna: A Ten Year Journey* (New York: Viking, 1990), 95. In this same interview the Dalai Lama is also said to have asserted that, according to the highest form of tantric Buddhism, it is understood that one can receive enlightenment in this lifetime, and that this is true for females as well as males.

131. Rita M. Gross, "The Feminine Principle in Tibetan Vajrayana Buddhism: Reflections of a Buddhist Feminist," *The Journal of Transpersonal Psychology* 16, no. 2 (1984): 179-80.

132. Ibid., 185.

133. Ibid., 186-90. For further discussion on feminism and Buddhism, see Rita Gross, *Buddhism After Patriarchy: A Feminist History, Analysis, and Reconstruction of Buddhism* (New York: SUNY Press, 1992).

134. Kaza, "Acting with Compassion," 53-62. Kaza also cites three areas in Buddhism which conflict with feminism. First, Buddhism sees the need to deconstruct the self; feminism sees the need to reclaim the self. Second, Buddhism lacks a power relation analysis, including the power issue in gender relationships; feminism offers a well-articulated power relation analysis. Third, Buddhism has an underdeveloped social justice ethic; feminism works at developing such an ethic (62-65).

135. Chatsumarn Kabilsingh, "Perception of Nature Project," World Wildlife Fund, presented at the Fourth International Buddhist-Christian Dialogue Conference, Boston University, July 31, 1992. While I have not previously perceived Kabilsingh as a feminist, recent information on the work she is doing on child and woman prostitution in South East Asia has caused me to change my mind.

136. El Saadawi, "Women and Islam," in *Women and Islam*, ed. al-Hibri, 193.

137. Leila Ahmed, *Women and Gender in Islam: Historical Roots of a Modern Debate* (New Haven: Yale University, 1992), 99-100. Ibn al-ᶜArabi was persecuted for his views in his lifetime but was too powerful intellectually to be ignored.

138. Annemarie Schimmel, "Women in Mystical Islam," in *Women and Islam*, ed. al-Hibri, 148-49. This citation is from *Mathnawī* (vol. 8, pp. 155ff.) by Ibn al-'Arabi.

139. Ahmed, *Women and Gender in Islam*, 42-43. It should be noted that

Ahmed's book pertains to Middle Eastern Arab women and focuses on the discourses about women and gender in those societies.

140. Ibid., 62.

141. El Saadawi, "Women and Islam," 194.

142. Ahmed, *Women and Gender in Islam*, 48.

143. Ibid., 58. The Käa'bà, which housed the Black Stone, a central symbol of tribal worship, became the primary site of Islamic pilgrimage and the worship of Allah.

144. Ibid., 3-4.

145. Ibid., 64-78.

146. Ibid., 88.

147. Ibid., 100-101. As more women are now being educated in Islamic societies, Ahmed expects the debates on interpretation of the laws to increase.

148. Ahmed, *Women and Gender in Islam*.

149. Ibid., 31.

150. Ibid., 30-33.

151. Riffat Hassan, "Muslim Women and Post-Patriarchal Islam," in *After Patriarchy*, ed. Cooey et al, 42.

152. Ibid., 41-44. The quotation is from page 44.

153. Ibid., 44-47.

154. Mernissi, *Beyond the Veil*, viii.

155. Ibid., xvi-xvii.

156. Mernissi, "Femininity as Subversion," in *Speaking of Faith*, ed. Eck and Jain, 95-108.

157. Ibid., 108.

158. Azizah al-Hibri, "A Study of Islamic Herstory: Or How Did We Ever Get into This Mess," in *Women and Islam*, ed. al-Hibri, 207. Al-Hibri suggests that the relationship of Islam and patriarchy may be seen in one of two ways: that Islam is a variation of patriarchal ideology; or that Islam, as the Word of God, transcends all ideologies. As the Word of God, there are also two options: as it stands, it is fair and just to women; as it is practiced today, it is patriarchal but not true Islam. In opting for the second possibility in both instances — that is, that Islam, as the Word of God, transcends all ideologies, and that Islam, as it is practiced today, is patriarchal but it is not true Islam — I see several difficulties. As the Word of God beyond ideologies, dialogue with other religions becomes impossible. Also, she seems to remove "true Islam" from any cultural context, which many, including other Muslims, would reject (cf., for example, Ahmed above).

159. Ahmed, *Women and Gender in Islam*, 88.

160. Quoted by el Saadawi, "Women and Islam," in *Women and Islam*, ed. al-Hibri, 201.

161. Ahmed, *Women and Gender in Islam*, 63.

162. Ibid., 188.

Index